Danny,
Prayi
Ore you + your family !
Lift your Gaze !

8-7-23

-26

Deep Waters:

Lift Your Gaze

Prayer Book

K. Clark

KIM M. CLARK

Books by Kim M. Clark

Enjoy reading these other books by Kim M. Clark, which are available on Amazon (scan the QR code under each book) and wherever fine books are sold:

Deep Waters:
Lift Your Gaze

Deep Waters: Lift Your
Gaze 30-Day Devotional

Aguas profundas:
¡Levanta tu mirada!
Devocional de 30 días

Endorsements

"I am twenty-five years into my life with Christ and I still feel like an infant in the arena of prayer. Maybe you feel the same way. Or maybe you are a "prayer warrior" who gets your highest joy from being in the presence of God in prayer. Either way, I believe you will find Kim M. Clark's *Deep Waters: Lift Your Gaze Prayer Book* to be a valuable resource to you. What Kim has done with this treasure is invite us to meet God on his terms, according to who he has revealed himself to be in the pages of Scripture. Enjoy reading, and more importantly, enjoy the fruit of a fresh approach to coming into the presence of God."

~ Chris Ogden, Pastor, Horizon West Church, Winter Garden, FL

"I am searching for words to describe the impact this prayer book has had on my life. If I use words like *transformation, intimacy, revelation,* and *empowerment,* they would do no justice to it. I do know that anyone who reads these prayers will be able to understand who we are and how we relate to our sovereign God. As a chaplain for incarcerated women, I am privileged to be able to share with our inmates a prayer book that, without a shadow of a doubt, will forever change their lives. Thank you, Kim, for allowing God to use you in such a mighty way!"

~ Chaplain Ivette Gonzalez, Orange County Jail Ministry
Orange County Jail, Orlando, FL

"When I first learned the Hebrew names of God more than forty years ago, it added a brand-new depth to both my personal walk with God, as well as ministry ability. This fantastic book by Kim M. Clark will introduce you to the very things that can add new meaning and impact for your prayer life. Kim also weaves so many terrific illustrations that make the truth come alive in a way that will help you to not just learn, but actually experience."

~ David Loveless, Executive Director, Campuses & Leadership Development
First Baptist Church, Orlando, FL

"A breathtaking book! Discover the power of praying God's Word and saying his holy name. *Deep Waters: Lift Your Gaze Prayer Book* will deepen and enrich your prayer life as it opens the channel for God to reveal his amazing grace and abundant blessings."

~ Jacquelyn Lynn, Author, *Finding Joy in the Morning* and *Words to Work By*

"Is there hope? That is one of the fundamental questions of life. Thankfully, the answer is yes! When we learn to go to the ultimate source of hope, we find hope and help from a loving heavenly Father who meets our every need. In Kim M. Clark's book *Deep Waters: Lift Your Gaze Prayer Book*, she introduces how God meets our deepest needs by showing us how to talk directly and intimately with God through the power of prayer."

~ Rodney Gage, Lead Pastor, ReThink Life Church, Orlando, FL Podcaster, and Author, *Family Shift* and *The Double Win*

"This book is AMAZING! Kim did not write a traditional book about God— she writes of a lifestyle and mindset change about who God is, how we view him, and how we can worship him. Kim truly breaks down each Hebrew name of God and his promises to us, as well as prayers that we can use in our lives. For an athlete to be successful on the playing field, they need to have a great training regimen and playbook. Kim created the training regimen and playbook on how to access God in our prayer life, as well as our daily lives. As someone recently hospitalized with COVID, prayers like these saved my life!"

~ Kevin Kendrick, Realtor & Founder, The Kendrick Team, Orlando, FL

"I love how God through his Holy Spirit inspires his people to help change a generation! He always begins with prayer through his holy Word. This amazing prayer book by Kim M. Clark, inspired by the Holy Spirit, does just that!

Whether you are one who struggles with prayer or one who loves to pray, it brings us all back to knowing who God is through his twelve revealed Hebrew names.

This book will teach, inspire, and push you to pray in ways you have yet to experience. It is an anointed on-time book for a generation who needs to know who our God is and how powerful our prayer lives become when we intimately know our God.

'But the people who know their God shall prove themselves strong and shall stand firm and do exploits [for God]' (Daniel 11:32 AMPC)."

~ Ray Valentin, Head Chaplain, Osceola County Jail

"This could be life-changing for those who struggle with their self-worth or are stuck in a rut with their stand-sit-kneel religious lifestyle. Break free and enter into communion with God. Learn how to pray his Word and speak his truths over you, your life, and your loved ones.

Kim M. Clark carefully sheds scriptural light on who God is to help you develop a deeper, more knowledgeable relationship with your Creator, who goes by many names."

~ Sally Friscea, Multiple-Award-Winning Coauthor, *Blessings in Disguise*

"This book is amazing. Well, Kim M. Clark's other ones are as well, but this one...Whoa. 'Anointed' is the perfect word."

~ Christy Distler, Multiple-Award-Winning Author, *A Cord of Three Strands* and *The Heart Knows the Way Home*

Dedication

This book is dedicated to those who have experienced
trauma—physically, emotionally, or spiritually.
My prayer is that our precious *Jehovah*
will draw near you,
heal your heart,
redeem you, and
pour out his mercy upon you and your family.

Contents

Prayer

noun

1: an address (such as a petition) to God in word or thought
2: the act or practice of praying to God[1]

Pray

intransitive verb

1: to make a request in a humble manner
2: to address God or with adoration, confession, supplication, or thanksgiving[2]

At the Table

"WORDS HAVE POWER. And *God's* words have unbelievable influence and authority. God used words to create the entire universe," I shared with my troubled friend as we sat down at my kitchen table to pray. "I pray Scripture to God in faith, knowing that his Word does not return void."

My girlfriend nodded. Her chair creaked as she shifted her weight.

I focused on the glimmer of curiosity in her bright blue eyes. "Remember when I couldn't go to that conference nearby and I had to attend the same event several states away on a different date? I prayed Romans 8:28 back to God and asked him to work that situation out for good. At that conference, I reconnected with a friend, shared the gospel with her, and she is now saved. She thanks me every time we talk, and praises God for preventing me from attending that event locally."

My friend's smile widened. "Ah, I remember that all too well. And I think I get it. You're praying God's promises in the Bible back to him, asking him to honor what he said."

"Exactly. Jesus Christ told us that we would do greater things than he did because Jesus is in heaven pleading to the Father for us."

"Whoa." She exhaled.

"I know, right?" I opened my hands wide in front of me, continuing, "God doesn't see me as the sinner that I am. Instead he hears my prayers as what they are—requests covered by the blood of his perfect, sinless, and righteous Son. It's not about *who's* praying—it's *how* we pray."

"I get it now. We know that the prayer of the righteous person is powerful and effective—and who's more righteous than Jesus?"

With a wide grin, I responded, "Bingo."

"Okay. I forgot who I was talking to. Let me change my prayer requests."

I laughed as I looked down at her long list of prayers in my prayer journal: to finish a project at work, exercise more, and eat healthier. "Sure, but why? Those are some good ones."

She smiled. "Because when *you* pray, God *moves*. I want to pray for BIG things!"

"Let's go, then!"

Exhaling, she poured out the deepest desires of her heart: to be married to a godly man, for victory over sin in her life, and for salvation for her family.

We bowed our heads and cried out to God with a renewed sense of faith. As we prayed, I felt that familiar deluge of warmth as the Holy Spirit cascaded over us—for whenever two or three come together in the name of Jesus, he is present (Matthew 18:20).

That conversation with my friend happened over a decade ago, and we are still seeing the fruit of those prayers. She is now married to a wonderful man, and most of her family members are saved. She still struggles with sin, just like we all do.

The great joy I experience when I pray and commune with God is my sustenance as a child of God. This intimacy is only available to those who have trusted in Jesus Christ as their personal Lord and Savior. If you haven't done that yet, take a moment and pray to yourself or out loud, "Jesus, I believe in you as my Savior. Forgive me for my sins. Come into my heart and save me."

Once we have taken that step of faith, God's Word becomes alive and active in our hearts and lives. Scripture now becomes sharper than any double-edged sword, penetrating our deepest recesses to divide soul and spirit, joints and marrow, and judging the thoughts and attitudes of the heart (Hebrews 4:12).

The Bible also becomes our most powerful offense and defense in our greatest battle—spiritual warfare (see Ephesians 6:10–18). Without the covering of the blood of Jesus, we are unarmed and defenseless for the spiritual war surrounding us. Only through praying to God, acknowledging that we are a sinner, asking forgiveness of our sins, and knowing that Jesus lived a sinless life and died on the cross for our sins, we are saved (see Romans 3–10). After declaring out loud that Jesus Christ rose from the dead and is our Lord and Savior, we now have access to the strongest force in the universe—a holy and perfect God (Romans 10:9–10). For there is only one way to the Father, and it's through faith in his Son, Jesus Christ, as our Lord and Savior (John 14:6).

When I pray Scripture in faith, I wield the mightiest weapon on earth. I have found that praying God's Word becomes profoundly more effective when I place my name in Scripture. In doing so, I have witnessed indescribable movements from God. These miracles are always, of course, in his perfect timing—not mine. I've often said that if we understood the power of God's Word, his promises, and his great love for us, our prayer life (along with the nature and results of our prayers) would change dramatically. Andrew Murray agrees:

> Beware in your prayer, above everything, of limiting God, not only by unbelief, but by fancying that you know what he can do. Expect unexpected things, above all that we ask or think. Each time you intercede, be quiet first and worship God in his glory. Think of what he can do, of how [God] delights to hear Christ, of your place in Christ; and expect great things.[3]

I encourage—no, I dare you—to pray God's words back to him. Throughout the following pages, read each prayer aloud and place your name in the blanks. This action is essential. When you insert your name into God's Word, you are declaring the source of all universal truth and authority over yourself, your heart's desires, and your life.

As I transcribed these personalized prayers from Scripture, the LORD spoke to my heart, "Since you are encouraging others to place the names I've given them into my Word, tell them of the meanings of my names as well."

In obedience to that revelation, I grouped the prayers under the twelve most common Hebrew names of God.[4] For the sake of simplicity, I used the Greek name for Jesus instead of the Hebrew name *Yeshua*, which means "God is Salvation" or "to deliver, save, or rescue."[5] And *Jehovah* for the transliteration of the Hebrew word for YHWH, or *Yahweh*, meaning "LORD" or "my God."[6] I also chose the more modern pointed (with vowels) instead of the unpointed Hebrew for the Names of God at the start of each section.

I found through my research that Jesus is the fulfillment of these names. Each chapter begins with an in-depth explanation of the twelve names of God. You can also visit the "Hebrew Names of God" section at the back of the book for a richer description of the Hebrew meaning of the root words for each Name of God.

The biblical order in which God revealed himself through his names shows a beautiful progression of intimacy while meeting the growing spiritual needs of his people.[7] Even more significant, every time you pray these personalized Scripture prayers or talk to God, you declare the meaning and promises of that name over your life.

Just as we have several names or titles (each having a different level of familiarity) for ourselves, so does God. For example, some of the names people call me (depending on our relationship) are "Child of God," "Mom," "Honey," "Mrs. Clark," "Miss Kim," "Sister," or "Daughter." I am also referred to based on my vocation, such as "author," "publisher," "speaker," "college instructor," "business owner," or "nonprofit founder."

Even the words of my full name, "Kim Marie Clark," have meaning. "Kim" signifies a leader, "Marie" alludes to someone who loves the sea, and "Clark" denotes a religious scholar or clerk. Each time I introduce myself, I reaffirm God's calling on my life as a leader, a lover of the ocean, and God's scribe. And when I speak my name within the ultimate supremacy of Scripture based on the Hebrew names of God, I am confirming and reminding myself of God's authority over and through me. I encourage you to research the meaning of your name as well. Know and own what God declares of you.

When you place your name in the blanks of this prayer book, feel the warmth of the Holy Spirit as you inhale his aroma, and allow yourself to experience God's delight in you as a follower of Jesus Christ. I encourage you to then recite these Scripture prayers again, this time with your loved ones' names in the blanks. Finally, a third time with the name of someone who has sinned against you. This last one is usually the most difficult—but the most powerful prayer of all. Speak the truth found in these prayers over you, your treasured family and friends, and yes, even your enemies.

Each of the twelve Hebrew names of God has seven supporting prayers—one for each day of the week—that depict and magnify that specific name of God, with a total of eighty-four petitions. You can recite one each day for twelve weeks or pray all the ones under that particular name of God in one sitting. Alternatively, if you are in a trial, I encourage you to keep reading until you feel encouraged and your gaze is lifted.

As I wrote and then prayed these personalized prayers over myself, I found myself weeping—the anointing is that strong. For me, I felt I was hearing the voice of God himself decreeing these words of comfort and blessing over me.

Afterward, stand back and watch God work (see Psalm 66:5). When God labors on our behalf, something extraordinary usually happens, and it's bigger and more incredible than anything we could ask or imagine. For even God declares, "So shall my word be that goes out from my mouth; it shall not return to me empty, but it shall accomplish that which I purpose, and shall succeed in the thing for which I sent it" (Isaiah 55:11 ESV).

After each personalized prayer, there are application questions based on each name of God—don't skip this section. Allow the Spirit of God to go deep into your heart to heal and transform it, making it more like his Son Jesus's. As I concentrate on God, remembering who I am praying to, my prayers are bolder and more passionate, and they produce more blessings than I could ever ask or imagine.

As another suggestion, try writing the desires of your heart with the dates in blue or black ink in a prayer journal and then record how God responds to your prayers in red (or another bright-colored) ink with the date(s) answered. You'll be encouraged as you look back upon these pages. When I review my prayer requests and answers with this simple technique, I am always in awe of God and how he moves. For me, this is the oxygen for my flames of faith, especially during times of intense difficulties and growth.

Pull up a chair to God's table of blessings he has already lavishly laid out for you in the presence of your enemies that is overflowing with his goodness, love, and mercy (see Psalm 23). For we don't wrestle against other people, but against spiritual powers, rulers, and authorities of darkness and evil (Ephesians 6:12).

Lastly, remember, God's got you, your loved ones, and yes, even your adversaries, in the palm of his hand. He's such a big God that he can even work sin out for good and his glory (see Romans 8:28).

Be blessed, my friend. And lift your gaze!

Names of God

BEFORE YOU START, here's a summary of the twelve Hebrew names of God we will be diving into as we decree God's promises through his Word over us, our loved ones, and even our enemies.

1. *Elohim:* God as the triune Creator, Ruler, and Sovereign over the universe, life, and all nations while promising the preservation of it all.
2. *Jehovah:* The LORD who is eternal, infinite, and self-existent and who only reveals this name to man who is made in his own image.
3. *El-Shaddai:* God Almighty who is the all-sufficient and satisfying One.
4. *Adonai:* Sovereign Lord or Master of our lives and service.
5. *Jehovah-Jireh:* Jehovah who has prevision and has provided the sacrificial Lamb for our redemption.
6. *Jehovah-Rophe:* Jehovah, the Healer of life's sickness, sorrows, and sins.
7. *Jehovah-Nissi:* Jehovah, my Banner, who is the provider of miracles for our victories over life's trials.
8. *Jehovah-M'Kaddesh:* Jehovah who sanctifies and sets his people apart for his possession and holy service.
9. *Jehovah-Shalom:* The Jehovah of our peace who reconciles us with Elohim.
10. *Jehovah-Tsidkenu:* Jehovah is the righteousness of people, which alone is the basis of their justification and acceptance.
11. *Jehovah-Rohi:* Jehovah my Shepherd.
12. *Jehovah-Shammah:* Jehovah is there.

~ 1 ~

ELOHIM

אֱלֹהִים

/El-lo-heem'/

Elohim Meaning

GOD | CREATOR | SUPREME POWER

I T IS MOST fitting that by the Hebrew name *Elohim*, God revealed himself as the triune Creator of the universe, as he brought the cosmos out of chaos, light out of darkness, existence out of barrenness, and life in his image.[8] This name, above all names, accurately refers to the Holy Trinity or the Godhead of three masculine beings (God, Jesus Christ, and Holy Spirit).

Some scholars believe the root of *Elohim* is *El*, which means mighty, strong, and prominent, or the incredible power of God. *Elohim* is, therefore, the ultimate divine creative and governing power, omnipotence (all-powerfulness), and sovereignty (in control of everything). The single verbal command of *Elohim* willed the vast universe into existence and, in doing so, guaranteed its redemption.[9]

As the Spirit of *Elohim* hovered over the deep waters before the formation of the earth (Genesis 1:2), *Elohim* created all things (including our planet and everything in it) through Jesus Christ (see Colossians 1:16). Jesus is also the object of God's love before the foundations of the world (see John 17:24) and shared in God's glory before the formation of the universe (see John 17:5).

The blessing and comfort from the name *Elohim* confirm the unbreakable contract or covenant relationship by his Son Jesus Christ, by whom *Elohim* is faithful to preserve his creation.[10] Thus everything in the universe proclaims to *Jehovah*, "You are my *Machseh* [refuge] and *Metsuha* [fortress], my *Elohim*, in whom I trust" (Psalm 91:2).

Elohim Scripture

In the beginning **Elohim** created heaven and earth. The earth was formless and empty, and darkness covered the deep water. The **Ruach Elohim** [**Spirit of Elohim**] was hovering over the water.

Then **Elohim** said, "Let there be light!" So there was light. **Elohim** saw the light was good. So **Elohim** separated the light from the darkness. **Elohim** named the light day, and the darkness he named night. There was evening, then morning—the first day.

Then **Elohim** said, "Let us make humans in our image, in our likeness. Let them rule the fish in the sea, the birds in the sky, the domestic animals all over the earth, and all the animals that crawl on the earth."

And **Elohim** saw everything that he had made and that it was very good. ~ Genesis 1:1–5, 26, 31

Elohim Prayers

ELOHIM, THE CREATOR

(Based on the promises in Genesis 1)

_____ is astounded by the awesome power of *Elohim*,
who in the beginning spoke the heavens and the earth into being.
_____, who is created in the image of *Elohim*—not just a physical
likeness, but also a spiritual personality and moral likeness—
is so thankful that the Father, Son, and Holy Spirit
created human beings, both male and female.
_____ is blessed by *Elohim* and rests in the authority that
humans have complete dominion over the fish of the sea,
the birds of the air, the cattle, and over the entire Earth,
and over everything that creeps and crawls on it.
_____ breathes life every moment of every day due to *Elohim*.
_____ is indebted to *Elohim*,
who commands for the provisions of
food, water, and protection for all of _____'s needs.
_____ is grateful to *Elohim* for creation.
_____ rejoices in the knowledge that when
Elohim looked over all he made,
including _____,
he declared everything
he made is very good.

Amen.

✝

ELOHIM INTIMATELY KNOWS ME

(Based on the promises in Genesis 1 and Psalms 91 and 139)

_____ is in awe of the all-powerful *Elohim*,

who at the beginning of Creation,

intimately knew _____.

_____ rests in the knowledge that

before the foundations of the earth were created

and the earth, moon, and universe were formed,

each detail of _____'s life and being was planned out by Elohim.

_____ rejoices that *Elohim* lovingly watched as

_____ was formed in the womb.

_____ knows that the power of *Elohim's* words has no equal.

_____ is astounded that *Elohim*

just spoke and everything was created.

Because _____ holds fast to *Elohim* in love, he/she does not fear.

_____ rests on the knowledge that *Elohim* delivers and protects his children.

_____ knows and worships *Elohim's* holy name.

_____ knows Elohim's Godhead is

made of three beings,

God, Jesus Christ, and Holy Spirit.

_____ breathes easily with the knowledge that he/she is loved by *Elohim*,

the Creator of the universe.

Amen.

†

ELOHIM AS JESUS CHRIST

(Based on the promises in John 1 and Genesis 17)

_____ rejoices that before anything was created,

the Word (Jesus Christ) and the Holy Spirit

co-existed eternally with the triune *Elohim*.

_____ acknowledges that only in Jesus Christ there is life.

_____ is in awe that all existence on earth

is the manifestation of *Elohim*.

_____ is grateful that the divine illumination

to reveal and impart life through

Jesus Christ shines into _____'s life.

_____ knows that the light of Jesus Christ overpowers

the world that is immersed in sin and stands in opposition to *Elohim*—

for the darkness cannot understand, correct, or absorb the Light.

_____ is more focused on *Elohim's* blessings

than on the actions, deeds, and words of others.

_____ is patient as *Elohim* works all things out for good and his glory.

Elohim confirms his promise of provision, love,

and care daily over _____ and

_____'s family, from generation to generation.

_____ is beyond blessed.

Amen.

†

ELOHIM IS OMNIPOTENT

(Based on the promises in Colossians 1)

_____ knows that Jesus is the visible living image of the unseen *Elohim*.

_____ declares that Jesus Christ is in *Elohim*.

_____ affirms *Elohim* as the Supreme One,

the Sovereign,

and the originator of all creation.

_____ knows *Elohim* existed before anything.

_____ rejoices that everything in heaven and on earth

—visible and invisible—

thrones or dominions or rulers or authorities,

was created through and for Jesus.

_____ acknowledges Jesus Christ, in *Elohim,*

is before all things,

and in Jesus Christ,

all things hold together.

_____ praises Jesus Christ as

the preeminent,

controlling, and

cohesive force of the universe.

_____ rests in the protective power of *Elohim*.

Amen.

†

ELOHIM'S GIFT OF RECONCILIATION

(Based on the promises in Colossians 1)

_____ confesses Jesus Christ is the head, life source, and leader of
the entire church and body of believers—past, present, and future.
_____ understands that Jesus is the beginning of everything,
including the firstborn from the dead.
_____ rejoices as *Elohim*, the Father, for all his
fullness—the total of his essence,
all his perfection, powers, and attributes—
permanently dwell in his Son, Jesus Christ.
_____ praises *Elohim,* who through the intervention of his Son,
reconciled everything to himself.
_____ celebrates that Jesus made peace with *Elohim* and
all believers in heaven and on earth through their faith in Jesus
and his complete work on the cross.
_____, who was once far away from, an enemy of, and
a hostile adversary to *Elohim* due to sin, is now a friend of *Elohim*.
As a result, _____ can now be brought into *Elohim's* presence
and _____ is seen as holy and blameless by *Elohim*.
_____ will stand before *Elohim* without a single fault.
_____ continues to believe the truth of the
gospel, stands firmly in its power, and
doesn't drift away from the assurance of the Good News.
_____ worships Jesus Christ, for reconciling him/her to *Elohim*.

Amen.

†

ELOHIM LOVES ME

(Based on the promises in Psalm 139)

_____ worships *Elohim* for making him/her so wonderfully complex!

_____ is in awe of *Elohim's* marvelous artistry.

Elohim delighted over _____ before he/she was born.

_____ is bathed in a spiritual waterfall of love from *Elohim*.

_____ realizes that *Elohim* watched as he/she

was being formed in utter secret,

intricately and skillfully knit together as if embroidered with many colors,

in the depths of the earth.

_____ breathes a sigh of relief,

knowing that every day of his/her life is

recorded in *Elohim's* book,

which is more binding than the strongest legal document.

All the days of _____'s life

were prepared before _____ even lived one day.

Elohim's highly valued purposes and thoughts

of _____ are so precious and many.

_____ can't even count them—they outnumber the grains of sand!

_____ praises *Elohim* every morning upon awakening.

Elohim is still on the throne!

Elohim is always with _____.

Amen.

✝

ELOHIM IS THE SUPREME POWER

_____ rejoices that by the Hebrew name *Elohim,*
God revealed himself as the triune Creator of the universe.
Elohim brought the cosmos out of chaos, light from darkness and barrenness, and
he created life in his image.

_____ celebrates that this name, above all names, accurately
refers to the Holy Trinity of the Godhead of three masculine
beings—God, Jesus Christ, and Holy Spirit.

_____ knows that the root of *Elohim* is *El,* which means
mighty, strong, and prominent, and the incredible power of God.

_____ worships *Elohim* as the ultimate divine creative
and governing authority, the only omnipotent (all-powerful)
and sovereign (in control of everything) being.

_____ is in awe of the power of *Elohim,* who, with a single
verbal command, willed the vast universe into existence
and, in doing so, guaranteed its redemption.

_____ is astonished by the power of the Spirit of *Elohim*
as he hovered over the deep waters before the formation of
the earth and created all things through Jesus Christ.

_____ exalts Jesus, who was the object of *Elohim's*
love before the foundations of the world.
Jesus also shared in *Elohim's* glory before the formation of the universe.

_____ receives the blessing and comfort from the name *Elohim,*
who confirms the unbreakable contract or covenant relationship
through his Son, Jesus Christ.

_____ and everything in the universe exclaims,
"*Elohim,* you are my refuge and fortress, in whom I trust."

Amen.

✝

My Prayers to Elohim

Ah, Lord GOD! It is you who have made the heavens and the
earth by your great power and by your outstretched arm!
Nothing is too hard for you. ~ Jeremiah 32:17 ESV

BEFORE WE PRESENT our prayer requests to our infinite and supreme
Elohim, let's take a moment to digest the immense authority that our
Elohim wields for us.

1. As we focus on *Elohim's* omnipotence, which means having unlimited
    power,[11] how does knowing that our *Elohim* is invincible and can do any-
    thing, change or alter your prayer requests?

    ----

2. How does knowing that you are praying to *Elohim*, who is sovereign and
    has infinite authority (meaning everything and everyone is under his
    control), comfort you?

    ----

3. List your prayer requests to your *Elohim*, who has the power to do **anything**, like speaking creation into reality:

_____

_____

_____

_____

4. Record your praises to your all-powerful *Elohim* even before he answers your prayers, despite your current situation:

_____

_____

_____

_____

5. How does knowing that Jesus Christ, part of your *Elohim*, died for you and will therefore not withhold any good gift from you (Romans 8:32), comfort you?

_____

_____

_____

_____

"Prayer is weakness leaning on omnipotence."[12] ~ W. S. Boyd

~ 2 ~

JEHOVAH

/Je-ho'-vah/

Jehovah Meaning

LORD | MASTER | REDEEMER

THE ENGLISH TRANSLATION of the transliteration of the Hebrew word YHWH is *Yahweh*, *Jehovah*, or LORD. This is the most used name for God in the Old Testament, occurring 6,823 times.[13] We will use the name *Jehovah* for the word for YHWH, which means "my God." This name refers to the Being who is absolutely self-existent, possessing life, and having a permanent existence. The base of *Jehovah* is the Hebrew verb *havah* which means "to be" or "life." *Jehovah* is the only name of God not based on an action. Instead, it is the "I AM WHO I AM" or "I WILL BE WITH YOU."

The name *Jehovah* was so sacred that the Israelites feared to even pronounce it—for death was the consequence for using or profaning this name. To this day, the name *Jehovah* is not read in synagogues, as it is considered too holy to be uttered.

Jehovah is also the name that God used upon making a special revelation of himself to his children.[14] The name connotates supremacy, absolute existence, and moral and spiritual righteousness.

Our only proper response to *Jehovah* is to fall down in terror, awe, and worship of the One who possesses all authority. *Jehovah* is holy and righteous; he grieves over our sins and responds with condemnation. Since *Jehovah* is also Love and *Jehovah-Jesus*, he therefore redeems us, continually seeking restoration of humankind back to himself.[15] *Jehovah's* existence, the continuity of his mercy in dealing with humans, the unchangeableness of his promises, and the whole revelation of redemption surrounds the loving name of *Jehovah*.[16]

Jehovah Scripture

Then **Yahweh** [Jehovah] **Elohim** formed the man from
the dust of the earth* and blew the breath of life into his
nostrils. The man became a living being. ~ Genesis 2:7

Elohim answered, "I will be with you. And this will be the
proof that I sent you: When you bring the people out of Egypt,
all of you will worship **Elohim** on this mountain."
Then Moses replied to **Elohim**, "Suppose I go to the people of Israel
and say to them, 'The **Elohim** of your ancestors has sent me to you,'
and they ask me, 'What is his name?' What should I tell them?"
Elohim answered Moses, "**Ehyeh** [I AM] Who **Ehyeh** [I AM]. This is what
you must say to the people of Israel: '**Ehyeh** [I AM] has sent me to you.'"
Again **Elohim** said to Moses, "This is what you must say to the people
of Israel: **Yahweh** [Jehovah] **Elohim** of your ancestors, the **Elohim** of
Abraham, Isaac, and Jacob, has sent me to you. This is my name forever.
This is my title throughout every generation." ~ Exodus 3:12–15

"You are my witnesses," declares **Yahweh** [Jehovah].
"I have chosen you as my servant so that you can know and believe
in me and understand that I am the one who did this. No god was
formed before me, and there will be none after me. I alone am **Yahweh**
[Jehovah], and there is no savior except me." ~ Isaiah 43:10–11

---

* There is a play on words here between Hebrew 'adam (man) and 'adamah (earth) source:
https://www.biblegateway.com/passage/?search=Genesis+2%3A7+&version=NOG, accessed 5-11-21.

Jehovah Prayers

JEHOVAH-ELOHIM, THE UNCHANGEABLE

(Based on the promises found in Deuteronomy 6;
Exodus 3; Isaiah 43; and Jeremiah 23)

The mighty *Jehovah* is _____'s *Elohim*.

_____ trusts explicitly in *Jehovah*,

the ever-existing, eternal, immutable,

and ever-becoming *Elohim*.

_____ loves *Jehovah-Elohim* with all of

his/her heart, soul, and strength.

_____ is so thankful that the same *Jehovah-Elohim*,

who revealed himself to Moses at the burning bush,

is his/her *Jehovah-Elohim*.

Jehovah is the name of _____'s *Elohim* forever

and is the same name _____ shall call on,

because, unlike man, *Jehovah* NEVER changes.

Jehovah is _____'s LORD, Master, and Redeemer.

_____ understands that *Jehovah* is

the one true living and all-supreme *Elohim*

and will never leave nor forsake _____.

Jehovah is _____'s

"I AM WHO I AM,"

"I WILL BE THAT BE," and

"I WILL BE WITH YOU."

Amen.

†

JEHOVAH, THE EVER-EXISTING ONE

(Based on the promises in Jeremiah 23 and Psalm 29)

_____ is in awe of *Jehovah*.

_____ rejoices because the great I AM [*Jehovah-Elohim*] is nearby.

_____ acknowledges that no one can hide from *Jehovah-Elohim*.

_____ praises *Jehovah* who fills the heavens and the earth.

_____ gives *Jehovah* all the glory due to his name.

_____ worships *Jehovah* in all the splendor of his holiness.

The speech of *Jehovah* is powerful and majestic—

it shatters the mighty cedars.

_____ is amazed as *Jehovah* makes the mountains skip like a calf

and the highlands leap like a young wild ox.

_____ is astonished as the voice of *Jehovah* strikes with bolts of lightning,

makes the barren wilderness quake, and

twists mighty oaks and strips the forests bare.

_____ joins the heavenly voices and

worships *Jehovah* as "the ever-existing One."

Jehovah rules over the floodwaters and reigns as King forever.

_____ is grateful to *Jehovah* for giving _____ strength.

Jehovah blesses _____ with peace.

Amen.

†

JEHOVAH, MY PROTECTOR

(Based on the promises found in Psalm 71)

_____ takes refuge in *Jehovah* and will never be put to shame.

_____ will be rescued and delivered by *Jehovah's* righteousness.

Jehovah is _____'s rock of refuge—the only true source of protection.

_____ knows *Jehovah* will save him/her, for *Jehovah* is _____'s fortress.

_____ trusts in *Jehovah* to rescue _____ from the hand of the wicked,

from the grasp of those who are evil and cruel.

Jehovah is _____'s hope and confidence.

_____ has become a remarkable display of

Jehovah's power, mercy, and grace to many.

_____'s mouth is filled with *Jehovah's* praise—

declaring *Jehovah's* splendor all day long.

_____ knows in old age, *Jehovah* will not cast away nor forsake him/her.

_____ trusts in *Jehovah*, who is never far away, to come quickly and help.

_____ fixates on *Jehovah*, while those who want to harm him/her

will be covered with scorn and disgrace.

_____ will always hope and praise *Jehovah's* saving acts all day long!

_____ proclaims *Jehovah-Elohim's* mighty acts and righteousness.

Jehovah-Elohim has taught and protected _____ since his/her youth.

Jehovah-Elohim does not forsake _____, even when he/she is old and gray.

_____ declares *Jehovah-Elohim's* power and

mighty acts to the next generation,

to all who are to come.

Amen.

†

JEHOVAH REDEEMS

(Based on the promises found in Psalm 71)

_____ praises the righteousness of *Jehovah-Elohim*,
which reaches to the heavens.
_____ declares *Jehovah-Elohim* as the One who has done great things.
_____ exclaims to all who will listen, "Who is like you, *Elohim*?"
_____ knows there is no one worthy of his/
her praises, except *Jehovah-Elohim*.
Even though *Jehovah-Elohim* has made _____ see troubles, many and bitter,
he/she has the faith and hope that *Jehovah-Elohim*
will restore _____'s life.
Jehovah-Elohim will again bring _____ up
from the depths of the earth.
Jehovah-Elohim will comfort _____ and make him/her greater than ever.
_____ will praise *Jehovah-Elohim* with
musical instruments for *Jehovah-Elohim's* faithfulness.
_____ will sing praises to *Jehovah-Elohim*.
_____'s lips will shout for joy.
_____ rejoices as his/her soul is redeemed and he/she is
now reconciled with *Jehovah-Elohim*.

Amen.
†

JEHOVAH IS FAITHFUL

(Based on the promises found in Psalm 112:1–9)

How joyful is _____ who fears *Jehovah*?

_____ exceedingly delights in obeying *Jehovah's* commands.

_____'s children will be successful everywhere—a

generation of godly people will be blessed.

Wealth and riches will be in _____'s home.

_____'s good deeds will last forever.

The light shines in the darkness for _____ and the godly.

_____ is generous, compassionate, and righteous.

Good comes to _____, who lends money

charitably and conducts business fairly.

_____ will not be overcome by evil.

_____ does not fear bad news because his/her

heart remains secure, trusting in *Jehovah*.

_____ is confident and will look triumphantly at all his/her enemies.

_____ shares freely and gives generously to those in need.

_____ will have influence and honor.

By the grace of *Jehovah*, _____'s head is raised in honor.

_____ trusts in *Jehovah* to protect him/her, despite his/her circumstances.

_____'s hope in *Jehovah* as his/her protector will never waver.

_____'s faith and salvation from declaring Jesus

Christ as his/her *Jehovah* are unwavering.

_____ rests in the knowledge nothing can separate _____ from *Jehovah*.

_____ knows that the Spirit of *Jehovah* is his/her source of comfort.

_____ praises *Jehovah* with all of _____'s heart.

Amen.

†

JEHOVAH, MY SAVIOR

(Based on the promises found in Psalm 18)

Jehovah is _____'s rock and Savior, in whom he/she takes refuge.

_____ rejoices as *Jehovah-Elohim's* name is honored above all other names.

_____ falls down in worship of *Jehovah-Elohim*, who can

mount on a mighty angelic being, and soar on the wings of the wind.

_____ trembles at the thoughts of

Jehovah-Elohim spreading apart the heavens and

coming down with dark storm clouds

beneath *Jehovah-Elohim's* feet.

_____ cries out to *Jehovah-Elohim* in distress.

Jehovah-Elohim heard _____'s cry for help.

_____ is so grateful as *Jehovah-Elohim*

reaches down from heaven,

draws him/her out of deep waters, and

rescues him/her from powerful enemies and

from those who are too strong for _____.

Jehovah-Elohim saves _____ because

Jehovah-Elohim delights in _____.

Jehovah-Elohim turns _____'s darkness into light.

Amen.

†

JEHOVAH, MY GOD

_____ knows that *Jehovah* can be called upon by many names, including the Hebrew word YHWH, *Yahweh*, *Jehovah*, or LORD.

_____ rejoices that this name is the most used name for God in the Old Testament, occurring almost seven thousand times.

_____ joyfully calls on the name *Jehovah*, or YHWH, which means "my God."

_____ understands this name refers to a Being who is absolutely self-existent, possessing essential life, and having a permanent existence.

_____ loves that the base of the name *Jehovah* is the Hebrew verb *havah*, which means "to be" or "life."

_____ receives comfort in the knowledge that *Jehovah* is the only name of God not based on an action—instead, it means "I AM WHO I AM" or "I WILL BE WITH YOU."

_____ realizes that *Jehovah* is the name that God used upon making special revelation of himself to _____ and his precious children.

_____ comprehends that the name *Jehovah* connotates supremacy, absolute existence, and moral and spiritual righteousness.

_____'s only response to *Jehovah* is to fall down in terror, awe, and worship of the One who possesses all authority.

_____ is grateful to *Jehovah*, who is also *Jehovah-Jesus*, because he redeems us, continually seeking the restoration of his children, including _____, back to himself.

_____ lovingly submits to the continuity of *Jehovah's* mercy, the unchangeableness of his promises, and the whole revelation of redemption surrounding the loving name of *Jehovah*.

Amen.

†

My Prayers to Jehovah

Don't you know? Haven't you heard?
El Olam [Everlasting], *Yahweh* [Jehovah], the Creator of the
ends of the earth, doesn't grow tired or become weary.
His understanding is beyond reach. ~ Isaiah 40:28

B EFORE WE POUR out our prayer requests to our *Jehovah*, the tireless Creator of the Universe, we need to remind ourselves to whom we are praying and why we have the assurance that our LORD, Master, and Redeemer hears us.

1. How does knowing you are praying to your *Jehovah*, which means everlasting or existing forever, without-end God,[17] alter your prayer request?

    _____

    _____

    _____

    _____

2. How does praying to your *Jehovah*, who has and will exist forever, comfort you?

    _____

    _____

    _____

    _____

    _____

3. How does the name-saving power of *Jehovah* reflect Jesus Christ? And how does that comfort you?

    _____

    _____

    _____

    _____

4. List your prayer requests to your *Jehovah*, who is everything—the Master of masters and LORD of lords:

    _____

    _____

    _____

    _____

5. Record your praises to your *Jehovah-Elohim* before your prayers are answered, despite your situation:

    _____

    _____

    _____

    _____

"Do we know the power of our supernatural weapon? Do we dare to use it with the authority of a faith that commands as well as asks? God baptizes us with holy audacity and Divine confidence." He is not wanting great men, but he is wanting men who will dare to prove the greatness of their God.
But God! But prayer!"[18]
~ A. B. Simpson

~ 3 ~

EL-SHADDAI

אֵל שַׁדַּי

/El-shad-di'/

El-Shaddai Meaning

THE TITLE *EL-SHADDAY* or *El-Shaddai* means "God Almighty." We'll use the more common translation of *El-Shaddai*. This Hebrew name for God signifies an all-bountiful being, the abundant source of all blessings. The name *El* denotes a God who is sure to help and who is supreme, unstoppable, and transcendent.

El-Shaddai refers to an all-powerful *Elohim* who compels nature to do what is contrary to itself to bless us abundantly.[19] This name also points to our *Elohim*, who lovingly prunes us to become more fruitful and filled to overflowing with his amazing fullness.[20] Every time we say *El-Shaddai*, we are reminded that our *El-Shaddai* is able to do and give exceedingly and abundantly more than we can ask or imagine.[21]

El-Shaddai declares that every good and perfect gift comes from him (James 1:17), and he never wearies in pouring out his mercies and blessings upon his people. The name *El-Shaddai* emphasizes that "his strength is made perfect in our weakness; his sufficiency is most manifest in our insufficiency; his fullness in our emptiness, that being filled, from us may flow rivers of living water to a thirsty and needy humanity."[22]

El-Shaddai is the name of our all-powerful, loving, and merciful God who empties us to overfill us with his unbelievable and unending eternal treasures, not the paltry wealth of men. This name also points to our Savior, Jesus Christ, who completely emptied himself on the cross so that our sins are forgiven and we may have life more abundantly.

El-Shaddai Scripture

When Abram was ninety-nine years old, the **LORD** [Jehovah] appeared
to him and said, "I am **El-Shaddai**—'God Almighty.' Serve me
faithfully and live a blameless life." ~ Genesis 17:1 NLT

"May *El-Shadday* [El-Shaddai] bless you, make you fertile, and increase
the number of your descendants so that you will become a community
of people. May he give to you and your descendants the blessing of
Abraham so that you may take possession of the land where you are
now living, the land that *Elohim* gave to Abraham." ~ Genesis 28:3–4

Elohim said to [Jacob], "I am *El-Shadday* [El-Shaddai]. Be fertile
and increase in number. A nation and a community of nations will
come from you, and kings will come from you." ~ Genesis 35:11

Elohim spoke to Moses, "I am *Yahweh* [**Jehovah**]. I appeared to Abraham,
Isaac, and Jacob as *El-Shadday* [El-Shaddai], but I didn't make myself
known to them by my name, *Yahweh* [**Jehovah**]." ~ Exodus 6:2–3

El-Shaddai Prayers

EL-SHADDAI, GOD ALMIGHTY

(Based on the promises found in Genesis 49 and Job 22)

_____ declares Jesus Christ as *Jehovah* and Savior.

Due to this declaration, _____ is blessed beyond measure.

_____ accepts instruction from *El-Shaddai's* mouth.

_____'s heart is full of *El-Shaddai's* words.

If _____ strays and then repents, he/she will

then be restored to *El-Shaddai*—

so _____ quickly turns from sin.

_____ glorifies *El-Shaddai* in all that _____ does, thinks, and prays.

_____ gives up the lust for money and no longer desires anything

more than *El-Shaddai* because he is _____'s treasure.

_____ takes delight in and prays continually to *El-Shaddai*.

_____ will succeed in whatever he/she chooses to do

through the strength and grace of *El-Shaddai*.

_____ has peace that *El-Shaddai* will shine a

light on the road ahead of him/her.

If people are in trouble and _____ prays for

them, *El-Shaddai* will save them.

_____ is in awe of the all-sufficient, all-powerful,

and all-bountiful *El-Shaddai*.

El-Shaddai exalts _____

with the blessings of the heavens above,

the blessings of the deep waters below,

and the blessings of comfort and compassion.

_____ worships *El-Shaddai*.

Amen.

†

EL-SHADDAI IS ETERNAL

(Based on the promises found in Psalm 68)

_____ rejoices that when *El-Shaddai* arises, his enemies scatter
and flee from his awesome presence.

_____ celebrates with joy and singing to *El-Shaddai*!

_____ exalts *El-Shaddai*, who rides on the clouds.

_____ praises *El-Shaddai*, a father of the
fatherless and a defender of the widows.

_____ is grateful to *El-Shaddai*, who places the lonely in families and
leads repentant prisoners out of incarceration into prosperity.

_____ is astonished that the earth shook and the heavens poured
down rain as *El-Shaddai* rescued his people from slavery in
Egypt, parted the Red Sea, and destroyed their enemies.

El-Shaddai sends abundant, refreshing, and
nourishing showers to fall on _____.

El-Shaddai sustains _____ when he/she is tired.

El-Shaddai is with _____.

Due to *El-Shaddai's* power over Creation,
_____ blooms wherever he/she is planted.

El-Shaddai provides for _____ from his incredible and vast bounty.

_____ joyfully blesses *El-Shaddai*, who bears his/her daily burdens and
is the *El* of _____'s salvation.

El-Shaddai delivers _____ from all evil.

Amen.

†

EL-SHADDAI IS BOUNTIFUL

(Based on the promises found in Ezekiel 1)

_____ is in awe of *El-Shaddai.*

_____ knows *El-Shaddai* is all-bountiful and

is the source of abundant blessings.

When _____'s faith wavers, _____ remembers *El-Shaddai,*

who is the all-powerful, without the limits of space and time.

_____ praises *El-Shaddai's* preeminence and

transcendence of all earthly constraints.

_____ knows the voice of *El-Shaddai* is like the tumult of a rushing army or

the synchronized movement of the thousands of angels' wings,

awaiting the mighty command from their *Elohim.*

_____ understands that *El-Shaddai's* words are

more power than rushing floodwaters.

_____ rejoices in *El-Shaddai's* omnipotence.

_____ understands that without a word, *El-Shaddai* can compel

nature to do what is contrary to its nature to bless _____.

Every time _____ says the name *El-Shaddai,*

_____ is reminded that *El-Shaddai* is

able to do abundantly and exceedingly

more than _____ can ask or imagine.

_____ loves to praise the name of the all-powerful *El-Shaddai.*

Amen.

†

EL-SHADDAI IS LOVE

(Based on the promises found in Ezekiel 10)

_____ is beyond grateful to *El-Shaddai*.

_____ comprehends that every good and

perfect gift comes from *El-Shaddai*.

_____ praises *El-Shaddai*, who never wearies in pouring out his tender,

new mercies and blessings each day on _____.

_____ trusts in *El-Shaddai*, even when *El-Shaddai* is pruning _____.

_____ knows that the act of pruning is one of love—making _____

a more accurate reflection of *Jehovah-Jesus*, the Son of *Elohim*.

_____ knows that through *El-Shaddai's* careful and perfect discipline,

_____ becomes even more fruitful.

_____ is indebted to *El-Shaddai* for _____'s flaws,

knowing that *El-Shaddai's* strength is made perfect in weakness.

_____ is thankful to the faithfulness of *El-Shaddai*,

who continually fills _____ to overflowing.

_____ understands that once he/she is filled,

rivers of living waters will flow from _____

to quench a thirsty humanity.

_____ rejoices that *El-Shaddai* cares so deeply and provides for _____.

Amen.

†

EL-SHADDAI IS FAITHFUL

(Based on the promises found in Exodus 6)

_____ rejoices because *El-Shaddai* is all-powerful and all-bountiful.

_____ has peace in the knowledge that *El-Shaddai*

has made a covenant and unbreakable relationship with _____.

_____ is thankful that *El-Shaddai* hears _____'s groaning,

secret prayer requests, and

hidden desires of _____'s heart.

El-Shaddai comforts _____ in times of affliction.

_____ worships *El-Shaddai* who delivers _____

from the bondage of slavery and

redeems _____ with a mighty outstretched arm.

_____ exalts *El-Shaddai* who takes _____ as one of his people.

_____ praises *El-Shaddai*, who has brought _____ out

from under the burdens and yoke of sin and oppression.

_____ is grateful to *El-Shaddai* for emptying and then

overfilling _____ with unbelievable and unending

eternal treasures, not the paltry riches of man.

_____ praises *Jehovah-Jesus*, who completely emptied himself out

on the cross so that _____'s sins are forgiven and _____ can

have life more abundantly than

he/she can ask or imagine.

Amen.

†

EL-SHADDAI, MY COVERING

(Based on the promises found in Psalm 91)

_____ resides in the protective shadow of *El-Shaddai*.

_____ declares *El-Shaddai* is a stronghold in whom _____ trusts.

_____ knows *El-Shaddai* will rescue _____ from any traps
and destructive plagues.

El-Shaddai will shelter and cover _____ with his feathers.

_____ finds safety under *El-Shaddai's* wings.

El-Shaddai's faithfulness is like a shield or a wall protecting _____.

_____ does not fear the terrors of the night, the arrow that flies by day,
the disease that stalks in the darkness, or the
destruction that ravages at noon because
_____ remains steadfast and trusts in *El-Shaddai*.

Though a thousand may fall beside _____, no harm will reach _____.

No destruction will overtake _____ and no illness
will come near _____'s home.

El-Shaddai will order his angels to protect _____ in all that he/she does.

They will lift up and carry _____ in their hands.

_____ will not slip and fall on a stone, or stumble.

El-Shaddai proclaims over _____,

"Because _____ is devoted to me, I will deliver _____;

I will protect and make _____ secure because he/she is loyal to me.

When _____ calls out to me, I will answer him/her.

I will be with _____ when he/she is in trouble;

I will rescue _____ and bring him/her honor.

I will satisfy _____ with long life.

_____ will see my salvation."

Amen.

†

EL-SHADDAI'S BLESSINGS

_____ rejoices that the Hebrew name *El-Shaddai*

means "God Almighty" and

signifies an all-bountiful being, the abundant source of all blessings.

_____ knows that the name *El* refers to a God who is sure to

help and who is powerful, omnipotent, and transcendent.

_____ worships *El-Shaddai* with the understanding that

this name describes an all-powerful *Elohim*

who commands the physical world to do what is opposite

to itself to care for, provide, and honor _____

more than he/she can ever ask or imagine.

_____ declares that every good and perfect gift comes

from *El-Shaddai* and he never wearies in

pouring out his mercies and blessings upon _____.

_____ is grateful to *El-Shaddai*,

whose strength has made _____ perfect in weakness,

whose sufficiency is most manifest in _____'s insufficiency,

and whose fullness is filled to overflowing in _____'s emptiness.

_____ praises the name of the all-powerful,

loving, and merciful *El-Shaddai*,

who pours out his unending eternal treasures over _____.

_____ knows that all these blessings are from _____'s Savior,

Jehovah-Jesus, who died on the cross so that

_____'s sins are completely forgiven and

_____ can boldly approach the throne of *El-Shaddai*.

Amen.

†

My Prayers to El-Shaddai

The sound of the angels' wings was heard as far as the outer courtyard. It was like the sound of **El-Shadday** [El-Shaddai] when he speaks. ~ Ezekiel 10:5

BEFORE WE POUR out our prayer requests to our *El-Shaddai*, who's voice is like the sound of thousands of angels' wings thundering, we need to remind ourselves to whom we are praying and why we have the assurance that our eternal, omnipotent, and bountiful Giver of Blessings hears us.

1. As we approach the throne of our *El-Shaddai*, which means "God Almighty," or God has unlimited power to do anything,[23] how does this knowledge change or alter your prayer request?

   _____

   _____

   _____

   _____

2. How does praying to *El-Shaddai*, who loves you enough to send his Son to die for you, comfort you?

   _____

   _____

   _____

   _____

3. List your prayer requests to your *El-Shaddai*, who is the ever-existent and ever-becoming One, meaning he has no end or beginning:

    _____

    _____

    _____

    _____

4. For you, how does the name *El-Shaddai* reflect Jesus Christ? And why does that comfort you?

    _____

    _____

    _____

5. Record your praises to your eternal *El-Shaddai*, God Almighty, and bountiful Giver of Blessings before he answers your prayers, despite your situation:

    _____

    _____

    _____

    _____

"Prayer is the slender nerve that moves the muscle of Omnipotence."[24]
~ Charles Spurgeon

~ 4 ~

ADONAI

אֲדֹנָי

/Ad-o-na'-i /

Adonai Meaning

MASTER OF MASTERS | LORD OF LORDS | MY LORDS'

THE HEBREW WORD *Adonai* translates as "Master" or "Lord," and is plural and possessive, or "my Lords'." The name *Adonai* signifies ownership or mastership, specifically expressing God's ownership of each member of the human family and requiring the absolute obedience of all humanity.[25] Accordingly, this lordship in God's name of *Adonai* encapsulates the complex yet loving relationship of God's possession of each person and the duty of our complete submission to our LORD.[26] Since *Adonai* is not an unjust Master, he doesn't ask what cannot be accomplished. When *Adonai* requires a task from his servants, he always equips his servants beforehand.[27]

In biblical times, the relationship between an Israelite master and a purchased slave or "bondservant" was a bond of endearment and much closer than the one of a hired servant. The slave was considered a family member and held a position of privilege so that a slave could partake in the Passover and have access to the holy things of the master's house, while the servant or stranger could not. And in the absence of a son, the slave was the heir of the master's entire household.[28]

Since man is born to worship and serve either *Elohim* or Satan, the day of *Adonai* is the day of reckoning for all men, whether or not they acknowledge *Jehovah* as their God.[29] Thankfully, Jesus Christ, our *Adonai*, who was and is the ultimate servant, will deliver all of us who have worked for, believed in, and trusted in Jesus as their Lord and Savior.

Adonai Scripture

Elohim understands the way to [wisdom].
He knows where it lives because he can see to the ends of the earth and
observe everything under heaven.
When he gave the wind its force and measured the water
in the sea, when he made rules for the rain and set paths
for the thunderstorms, then he saw it and announced it.
He confirmed it and examined it. So he told humans,
"The fear of *Adonay* [**Adonai**] is wisdom!
To stay away from evil is understanding." ~ Job 28:23–28

There is no one like *Yahweh* [**Jehovah**]—your one true
Elohim and *Adonay* [**Adonai**]. He is the great, powerful, and
awe-inspiring *El*. He never plays favorites and never takes a bribe.
He makes sure orphans and widows receive justice. He loves foreigners and
gives them food and clothes. So you should love foreigners,
because you were foreigners living in Egypt. Fear *Yahweh* [**Jehovah**]
your *Elohim*, worship him, be loyal to him, and take your oaths
in his name. He is your glory. He is your *Elohim*, who did
for you these spectacular and awe-inspiring deeds you
saw with your own eyes. ~ Deuteronomy 10:17–21

Yahweh [**Jehovah**] said to my Lord [**Adonai**], "Sit in the highest position
in heaven until I make your enemies your footstool." ~ Psalm 110:1

O *Yahweh* [**Jehovah**], our *Adonay* [**Adonai**], how majestic is your name
throughout the earth! Your glory is sung above the heavens. ~ Psalm 8:1

Adonai Prayers

ADONAI IS MAJESTIC

(Based on the promises found in Psalm 8 and Mark 14)

Adonai's name is majestic and declared throughout
the earth, and his glory is eternal.
_____ knows he/she is under the protection of his/her Master, *Adonai*.
Adonai builds a fortress against his opponents and silences the enemy.
When _____ looks to the heavens, the creation of *Elohim's* fingers,
and sees the moon and the stars that *Elohim* has set in place—
_____, a meager human, wonders how *Elohim*
even remembers and cares for _____.
_____ is in awe of *Elohim*, who has made humanity a little lower
than the angelic beings and crowned humans with glory and honor
to rule everything that *Elohim's* amazing hands have created.
Jehovah-Adonai is magnificent!
_____ is indebted to *Jehovah-Jesus,* who in the moments
of agony before his crucifixion, begged his Abba to take
the cup of wrath for all humanity's sins from him.
Instead, Jesus, the Son of *Elohim,* took all of _____'s
sins on the cross and paid for them in full so that _____
could approach *Elohim's* holy throne of grace.
Because of *Jehovah-Jesus's* sacrifice on the cross and triumph over death,
Adonai hears _____'s prayers and
will never leave, nor forsake him/her.
_____ worships *Jehovah-Adonai*.

Amen.

†

ADONAI PROTECTS ME

(Based on the promises found in Psalm 16)

_____ praises *Adonai* for keeping _____ safe.

_____ has found shelter under the protection of *El-Shaddai*.

_____ knows that without *Jehovah-Adonai*,

_____ has nothing good.

_____ acknowledges that those who lead holy lives

are filled with joy and

those who chase after other worries of the world have sorrow.

Jehovah-Adonai is _____'s inheritance, stability, and prosperity.

_____ knows that *Jehovah* is the one

who makes his/her future secure.

Jehovah-Adonai is always guiding _____.

Adonai is at _____'s right hand—he/she is not shaken or fearful.

_____'s heart rejoices in *Adonai*.

_____ is safe and secure.

Adonai's boundary lines fall in pleasant places.

_____ experiences absolute joy and

sheer delight in *Adonai's* presence.

_____'s legacy is beautiful.

Amen.

†

ADONAI, MY TEACHER

(Based on the promises found in Psalm 16)

Elohim protects _____.

_____ takes refuge in *Elohim.*

Adonai is _____'s *Jehovah.*

Adonai advises _____.

Adonai instructs and teaches _____ each day and night.

Because _____ has set *Adonai* in front of him/her,

_____ rests and sleeps peacefully.

_____ knows that *Adonai* is by his/her side and

he/she cannot be moved.

That is why _____'s heart and

soul rejoices.

_____ is thankful *Adonai* will not abandon him/her.

Adonai makes the path of life known to _____.

_____ breathes a sigh of relief that the abundance of

joy and eternal pleasures

are the result of being in

Adonai's presence.

_____ praises *Adonai.*

Amen.

†

ADONAI, MY ROCK

(Based on the promises in Psalm 62)

_____ praises *Adonai*, his/her Master.

_____ waits calmly for *Adonai*

because all _____'s hope comes from *Adonai*.

Adonai is _____'s rock and Savior.

_____ cannot be shaken.

Adonai is _____'s stronghold.

_____ knows that salvation and glory

come only from *Adonai*.

Adonai is the source of _____'s strength.

_____ trusts in *Adonai* at all times.

_____ pours out his/her heart to *Adonai*.

_____ recognizes that people, even important ones,

are only a whisper in the wind—a delusion—compared to *Adonai*.

When riches increase, _____ does not depend on them.

_____ knows that all power and mercy belong to *Adonai*.

_____ praises *Adonai* for his infinite and underserved

compassion, love, and salvation.

Adonai is _____'s *Jehovah* and Master.

_____ is grateful to *Adonai* for saving _____

through the perfect work of *Jehovah-Jesus* on the cross.

Amen.

†

ADONAI-JEHOVAH

(Based on the promises found in Deuteronomy 3 and Jeremiah 32)

_____ worships *Adonai-Jehovah*.

_____ knows that *Adonai-Jehovah* has only begun to

show his extraordinary power, greatness, and mighty hand.

There are no other gods in heaven or on earth that can perform

the works and miracles of

Adonai-Jehovah.

_____ understands that *Elohim* made the heavens and the Earth.

Nothing is too hard for _____'s *Adonai-Jehovah*.

_____ rejoices because *Adonai-Jehovah* shows

mercy to thousands of generations.

Adonai-Jehovah is great and mighty.

_____ worships *Adonai-Jehovah* who protects and watches over him/her.

_____ is not afraid.

_____ has peace that *Adonai-Jehovah* will fight for _____.

_____ rejoices because *Adonai-Jehovah* is

the *Elohim* of all flesh and nothing is too hard for him.

_____ rests on the knowledge that *Adonai-Jehovah* cares and

provides for _____ and all his/her needs.

_____ enjoys all the privileges of having *Adonai-Jehovah* as his/her Master.

_____ is well taken care of and provided for by *Adonai*.

_____ praises *Adonai*.

Amen.

†

ADONAI, MY DEFENDER

(Based on the promises found in Psalm 35)

Adonai is _____'s defender.

Adonai opposes and fights against those who are against _____.

Adonai gives _____ the victory.

_____ understands that *Adonai* will bring shame and disgrace
on those trying to harm him/her.

Adonai can blow away _____'s enemies like chaff in the breeze or
a wind sent by one of the mighty angels.

Adonai can make _____'s opponents' path dark and slippery,
as the angel of *Adonai* pursues them.

Adonai rescues _____ when he/she is helpless.

Adonai thwarts the plans of _____'s enemies.

Even when _____ is being attacked and slandered,
Adonai protects _____.

Adonai helps _____ forgive those who
have profoundly and painfully betrayed _____.

Adonai vindicates and protects _____.

_____ praises *Adonai* with every bone in his/her body.

Adonai is _____'s defender.

Adonai delights in blessing and
protecting his servant, _____, with peace.

Amen.

†

ADONAI, MY MASTER

Adonai is _____'s Master.

_____ is a servant of *Adonai*.

Adonai intercedes for _____.

Adonai does not forsake his own.

_____ rejoices that *Jehovah-Jesus*

paid such a great price

for _____'s life.

Elohim treasures _____ so much

that it is beyond _____'s understanding.

_____ knows that the very name of *Adonai*

signifies blessed ownership, care, and protection of _____.

_____ joyfully obeys *Adonai*, even when _____ is afraid.

Adonai lovingly watches over and views _____ as his beloved child.

_____ knows *Adonai* is not an unjust Master and

Adonai always equips his servants, like _____,

before assigning them a task.

Adonai will never ask _____ to perform an

assignment that _____ is not able to do.

_____ rests in the knowledge that

_____ is in the family of *Adonai*

through the blood of *Jehovah-Jesus*.

_____ is secure in the knowledge that as a slave of *Adonai*,

_____ is an heir of the entirety of his/her Master's eternal household.

_____ worships *Jehovah-Adonai*.

Amen.

†

My Prayers to Adonai

"Behold, I am Jehovah, the God of all flesh: is there
anything too hard for me?" ~ Jeremiah 32:27 ASV

BEFORE WE POUR out our prayer requests to our *Adonai*, who is the God
of all flesh, we need to remind ourselves to whom we are praying and
why we have the assurance that our LORD of lords, the Master of masters,
delights in our prayers.

1. How does resting in the knowledge that our amazing *Adonai* loves you
    as much as his own Son and does not withhold any good gift from you,
    change or alter your prayer request?

    _____

    _____

    _____

    _____

2. How does praying to your *Adonai*, who always equips his servants for the
    task he calls us to beforehand, encourage you?

    _____

    _____

    _____

    _____

3. List your prayer requests to your *Adonai*, your Master and Lord, who will never leave nor forsake you:

    _____

    _____

    _____

    _____

4. List your praises to your *Adonai*, who takes ownership of your provision, care, and needs before your prayers are answered, despite your situation:

    _____

    _____

    _____

    _____

5. How does Jesus, who said we would perform greater miracles than he did, and is the ultimate example as the ultimate servant of *Adonai*, comfort you?

    _____

    _____

    _____

    _____

    _____

> "The one concern of the devil is to keep Christians from praying.
> He fears nothing from prayerless studies, prayerless work and
> prayerless religion. He laughs at our toil, mocks at our wisdom,
> but he trembles when we pray."[30] ~ Samuel Chadwick

~ 5 ~

JEHOVAH-JIREH

/Je-ho'-vah Yeer'eh/

Jehovah-Jireh Meaning

THE LORD WHO FORESEES AND PROVIDES

THE NAME OF *Jehovah-Jireh* not only means the LORD who provides, but also the God who foresees. The Hebrew word *Jireh* is simply the form of the verb "to see," but compounded with the *Jehovah* or the "One who possesses all wisdom and knowledge who foresees everything from eternity to eternity," it means "to see beforehand" or have prevision.[31] Thus *Jehovah-Jireh's* provision and prevision are the same thing. He, therefore, provides for us before we even know we have the need. Our *Jehovah-Jireh* delivers yesterday, today, and tomorrow, for his provisions are continual and unending.

Abraham, during his greatest trial, first uttered this Hebrew name of God in Genesis 22 on Mount Moriah. In the final moment when Abraham was ready to sacrifice his only beloved and promised son, Isaac, *Jehovah's* angelic messenger spoke, telling Abraham not to lay a hand on his son. Abraham's faith was tested and he passed. This is the same mountain that "became the site of Calvary and the scene of that grand and awful sacrifice of God's only-begotten and well-beloved Son, who was put under judgment for sin, and became our Substitute."[32]

Our *Jehovah-Jireh* meets our eternal needs as well. He provided the perfect and sinless Lamb of sacrifice for all of our sins—his one and only beloved Son—so that we can be reconciled with our *Elohim* through our faith. How much more will he then provide for us, who are covered, illuminated, and redeemed by the invaluable blood of his Son? Exceedingly and abundantly more than we can ever ask or imagine. That is our *Jehovah-Jireh*.

Jehovah-Jireh Scripture

Then Abraham took the wood for the burnt offering and
gave it to his son Isaac. Abraham carried the burning coals
and the knife. The two of them went on together.
Isaac spoke up and said, "Father?"
"Yes, Son?" Abraham answered.
Isaac asked, "We have the burning coals and the wood,
but where is the lamb for the burnt offering?"
Abraham answered, "**Elohim** will provide a
lamb for the burnt offering, Son."
The two of them went on together.
When they came to the place that **Elohim** had told him about, Abraham
built the altar and arranged the wood on it. Then he tied up his son Isaac and
laid him on top of the wood on the altar. Next, Abraham picked up the knife
and took it in his hand to sacrifice his son. But the Messenger of **Yahweh**
[**Jehovah**] called to him from heaven and said, "Abraham! Abraham!"
"Yes?" he answered.
"Do not lay a hand on the boy," he said. "Do not do anything
to him. Now I know that you fear **Elohim**, because you
did not refuse to give me your son, your only son."
When Abraham looked around, he saw a ram behind him
caught by its horns in a bush. So Abraham took the ram and
sacrificed it as a burnt offering in place of his son.
Abraham named that place **Yahweh Yireh** [**Jehovah-Jireh**].
It is still said today,
"On the mountain of **Yahweh** [**Jehovah**] it will be provided."
~Genesis 22:6–14

79

Jehovah-Jireh Prayers

JEHOVAH-JIREH IS FAITHFUL

(Based on the promises found in Genesis 28)

_____ knows everything in heaven and on earth is connected.

_____ is thankful to *Jehovah* who gives _____ dreams.

_____ knows it was *Jehovah* who gave Jacob the dream of

a stairway with *Elohim's* angels going up and down it,

interconnecting heaven and earth.

_____ is grateful to *Jehovah*.

Jehovah is faithful to watch over _____

wherever _____ goes.

_____ knows *Jehovah-Jireh*

will always provide whatever _____ requires,

because _____'s *Jehovah-Jireh* presees and prevides for

all of _____'s needs

before _____ even realizes it.

_____ understands *Jehovah-Jireh*

will never leave, nor forsake _____.

Jehovah-Jireh will bring to

fruition all that he has promised _____.

Jehovah-Jireh will completely and abundantly provide for _____.

_____ praises *Jehovah-Jireh*.

Amen.

†

JEHOVAH-JIREH, MY DELIVERER

(Based on the promises found in 1 Samuel 2)

_____ rejoices because *Jehovah* delivers _____.

_____'s heart finds joy in *Jehovah-Jireh*.

_____'s gaze is lifted and locked on *Jehovah-Jireh*.

_____ knows that there is no one like his/her *Jehovah-Jireh*.

_____'s *Jehovah* is an *El* of knowledge,

and *Jehovah* weighs all of our actions.

_____ trusts in *Jehovah-Jireh* who protects _____.

_____'s *Jehovah* breaks the weapons of the wicked.

Jehovah-Jireh will fortify _____ with strength.

Jehovah-Jireh provides life, causes poverty, and grants wealth.

_____ knows it is *Jehovah-Jireh* who humbles people and promotes them.

Jehovah-Jireh lifts the needy from the trash to make them sit with nobles and

has them inherit a glorious throne.

_____ acknowledges that the pillars of the earth are *Jehovah's*.

Jehovah-Jireh safeguards the steps of his faithful ones, like _____.

_____ understands *Jehovah* silences wicked people in darkness.

_____ knows that people cannot succeed by their own strength;

it is only through *Jehovah-Jireh*.

Jehovah-Jireh provides _____ with strength, power, and faith.

_____ praise *Jehovah-Jireh*.

Amen.

†

JEHOVAH-JIREH STRENGTHENS

(Based on the promises found in Isaiah 25, 40, and 61)

_____ is grateful that *Jehovah-Jireh* is a guard for the helpless,
a defense for the needy in distress, and a refuge from the storm.
_____ recognizes the breath of the ruthless
is like a rainstorm against a wall,
they are no match for *Jehovah-Jireh.*
_____ worships *Jehovah-Jireh* who grants those who grieve peace,
giving them a garland of blessings instead of ashes,
the oil of gladness instead of mourning, and
the mantle of praise instead of a spirit of fainting
so they will be called oaks of righteousness planted by *Jehovah.*
_____ has peace because *Jehovah-Jireh's* understanding is beyond reach.
_____ knows it is *Jehovah-Jireh* who increases _____'s energy
when _____ is weak.
_____ waits upon *Jehovah-Jireh* for strength.
_____ understands that everyone gets fatigued and
even young people will stumble and fall.
_____ waits with hope for the faithful *Jehovah-Jireh,* who presees.
_____'s strength will be renewed because of
Jehovah-Jireh's protection, faithfulness, and prevision.
_____ will soar on wings like eagles and will
run and will not become weary.
_____ will walk and will not grow tired.

Amen.

†

JEHOVAH PROVIDES ALL THINGS

(Based on the promises found in Exodus 16; Deuteronomy
2; 1 Kings 17; 1 Kings 19; and Mark 6 and 8)

_____ is so grateful that _____'s *Jehovah-Jireh* is the same *Jehovah*
who provided manna every morning for forty years to the Israelites
when they were in the wilderness, despite their sin and complaining.
_____ knows of the continual blessings and care that *Jehovah-Jireh,* who
showered down upon Elijah when the ravens
brought him bread and meat in the mornings and evenings,
will also provide sustenance for _____ and _____'s family.
Even when _____ is frightened like Elijah
when he was running in fear for his life from his enemy, Jezebel,
_____ trusts in *Jehovah-Jireh* to protect _____ because
Jehovah-Jireh presees all of _____'s needs and
provides for _____ in advance.
_____ praises *Jehovah-Jireh* because he delivers _____
the same way *Jehovah* fed the multiples through the
obedience and prayers of Elisha and *Jehovah-Jesus.*
For thousands ate and were satisfied, and they had copious leftovers.
That same *Jehovah-Jireh* will abundantly provide for
_____ and _____'s family through _____'s prayers.
_____ rejoices as *Jehovah-Jireh* has
blessed _____ in everything _____ has done.
Elohim has always been near _____ during
_____'s darkest days and wanderings.
As a result of *Jehovah-Jireh's* prevision,
_____ has not needed or lacked a thing.

Amen.

†

JEHOVAH WHO PRESEES

(Based on the promises found in Job 34; and Psalms 32, 68, and 113)

_____ rejoices for *Jehovah-Jireh* presees all of _____'s needs.
_____ knows that *Jehovah-Jireh's* eyes are always
upon the ways of each man and woman.
Jehovah-Jireh sees all of _____'s steps and everyone else's,
whether in the past, present, or future.
_____ praises *Jehovah-Jireh*, whose mercy and
glory are higher than all the heavens.
The streams of _____'s life are like *Elohim's* rivers which are full
of water that drench the groves of the land, settling its ridges.
The waters of _____'s *Jehovah-Jireh* softens the dirt,
quenching its thirst with bountiful showers.
_____ knows *Jehovah-Jireh* blesses all the vegetation
and crowns the year with immeasurable bounty—for all
of *Jehovah-Jireh's* paths drip with abundance.
Jehovah-Jireh's goodness and provision drop sustenance
over the meadows in the wilderness, and the hills rejoice.
_____'s pastures overflow and the hills are robed with delight.
_____'s valleys are covered with grain and they
shout for joy and sing praises to *Elohim*!
Jehovah-Jireh is a Father to the fatherless and
a Judge of the widows and orphans.
Jehovah-Jireh provides goodness and protection for the poor.
_____ acknowledges *Jehovah-Jireh* as _____'s *Elohim*, who is enthroned
on high and knows all things that are in heaven and on the earth.
_____ has comfort that *Jehovah-Jireh* will instruct and teach
_____ in the way which he/she should go.
Jehovah-Jireh provides _____ with solid counsel and
watches over _____.

Amen.

✝

JEHOVAH-JIREH'S BLESSINGS

(Based on the promises found in 1 Chronicles 17 and 29; Psalms 5 and 65;
Ezekiel 34; and Matthew 6)

_____ praises *Jehovah-Jireh* for appointing a place to plant _____,

so that _____ may dwell in a place of his/her own and move no more.

And _____'s enemies will no longer oppress _____ and _____'s family.

_____ exalts *Jehovah-Jireh* alone,

who holds the authority to make people, places, and all things great.

Jehovah-Jireh strengthens _____.

_____ knows *Jehovah-Jireh* blesses _____ and

surrounds _____ with favor as with a shield.

_____ is amazed at the power of *Jehovah-Jireh*,

who causes the vapors to ascend from the ends of the earth,

makes lightning for the rain,

and brings forth the wind from *Elohim's* treasuries.

Jehovah-Jireh showers blessings upon _____ and

will cause rain to come down when _____ needs water.

Jehovah-Jireh promises _____'s trees will

produce their fruit in season and will increase in yield.

Everyone around _____ will know that *Jehovah-Jireh* provides for _____.

Jehovah-Jireh will deliver _____ from the hand

of those who have enslaved _____.

_____ praises *Jehovah-Jireh* who will raise a garden of renown for _____,

so _____ will no longer be consumed with hunger and want.

_____ will be secure in the land.

_____ praises *Jehovah-Jireh*.

Amen.

†

JEHOVAH-JIREH IS UNCHANGEABLE

(Based on the promises found in Genesis 22)

_____ understands *Jehovah-Jireh's* provision
and prevision are the same thing.
Jehovah delivers yesterday, today, and tomorrow,
for *Jehovah-Jireh's* provisions for _____ are continual and unending.
Just as *Jehovah-Jireh* was faithful to Abraham during his
greatest trial, the prevention of the sacrificial offering of his son
Isaac, the unchangeable *Jehovah-Jireh* is loyal to _____.
As *Jehovah-Jireh* tried Abraham, _____ understands that
when *Jehovah-Jireh* tests _____'s faith, it is for _____'s
spiritual growth, sanctification, and *Jehovah's* glory.
_____ is beyond grateful that on the same mountain that an
angel of *Elohim* prevented Abraham from offering his beloved
and promised son, Isaac, *Jehovah-Jireh* sacrificed of his
only-begotten and well-loved Son, *Jehovah-Jesus,* for _____.
_____ praises *Jehovah-Jesus,* who received the entire judgment and penalty
for _____'s sin and became _____'s Substitute.
_____ rejoices now that he/she is reconciled with
Elohim through _____'s faith in *Jehovah-Jesus.*
Jehovah-Jireh has provided eternally for _____,
who is covered, illuminated, and redeemed by the
invaluable blood of *Jehovah-Jesus,*
and *Jehovah-Jireh* will not withhold any good gifts from _____.
_____ exalts *Jehovah-Jireh,* who meets all of _____'s needs:
eternal, physical, emotional, or spiritual.

Amen.

†

My Prayers to Jehovah-Jireh

"No weapon forged against you will prevail, and you will refute every tongue that accuses you. This is the heritage of the servants of the Lord, and this is their vindication from me," declares the LORD. ~ Isaiah 54:17 NIV

BEFORE WE POUR out our prayer requests to our *Jehovah-Jireh*, we need to remind ourselves to whom we are praying and why we have the assurance that our *Jehovah-Jireh*, who will alter the laws of nature to provide for us, will never leave us nor forsake us.

1. How does knowing that our *Jehovah-Jireh* has prevision and sees our needs before we even know we have them, change or alter your prayer request?

   _____

   _____

   _____

   _____

2. How is our faith in *Jehovah-Jireh* glorified, especially to unbelievers watching us, when we pray to our *Jehovah*, who has prevision?

   _____

   _____

   _____

3. List your prayer requests to your *Jehovah-Jireh*, who abundantly supplies more than we can ask or imagine:

4. List your praises in advance to your *Jehovah-Jireh*, who provides for you before you even ask your petitions, despite your situation:

5. How does knowing that *Jehovah-Jireh* has already provided *Jehovah-Jesus* to meet our greatest need comfort you and change your prayer request?

"I strongly suspect that if we saw all the difference even the tiniest of our prayers to God make, and all the people those little prayers were destined to affect, and all the consequences of those effects down through the centuries, we would be so paralyzed with awe at the power of prayer that we would be unable to get up off our knees for the rest of our lives."[33] ~ Dr. Peter Kreeft

~ 6 ~

JEHOVAH-ROPHE

יְהֹוָה רֹפֵא

/Je-ho'vah Ro'-phay/

Jehovah-Rophe Meaning

THE LORD WHO HEALS AND RESTORES

THE NAME *JEHOVAH-ROPHE* points to our *Jehovah*, who heals and redeems. This Hebrew name of God was first introduced as the millions of Israelites fled the oppression of slavery in Egypt. After witnessing *Jehovah's* miraculous parting of the Red Sea and then the drowning of their enemies under the great swells of the mighty waters, the Israelites wandered in the desert for three days without water. This purification process drained them—making them irritable, thirsty, and spiritually dehydrated. They loudly protested to Moses, their leader. When they found water in Marah, it was bitter and undrinkable. Then our great *Jehovah* showed Moses a tree, which when thrown into the spring, made the water potable.

The complaining Israelites wandering in the desert foreshadows us wallowing in our sin. The water represents our greatest need—access to *Elohim*. The tree symbolizes our Savior, who on a wooden cross, became sin for the salvation of all humanity. The *Jehovah-Rophe* who heals in the Old Testament is the same *Jehovah-Jesus* who restores in the New Testament.[34]

Jehovah-Rophe cures us of our physical ailments but does so much more. This is the name of the One who rescues and heals, and who alone possesses the remedy for our greatest disease—sin. Through Christ, our *Jehovah-Rophe* has sweetened the bitterness of human misery and death. This name affirms our access to the living waters that only flow from *Jehovah-Jesus*, while boldly declaring our spiritual reconciliation with our *Jehovah-Elohim*.

Jehovah-Rophe Scripture

So Moses cried out to the LORD [Jehovah] for help, and
the LORD [Jehovah] showed him a piece of wood. Moses threw
it into the water, and this made the water good to drink.
It was there at Marah [which means bitter] that
the LORD [Jehovah] set before them the following decree
as a standard to test their faithfulness to him.
He said, "If you will listen carefully to the voice of the LORD [Jehovah] your
God [Elohim] and do what is right in his sight, obeying his
commands and keeping all his decrees, then I will not make you
suffer any of the diseases I sent on the Egyptians; for I am the LORD
[Jehovah-Rophe] who heals you." ~ Exodus 15:25–26 NLT

The moon will be as bright as the sun, and the sun will be seven
times brighter—like the light of seven days in one! So it will
be when the LORD [Jehovah-Rophe] begins to heal his people
and cure the wounds he gave them. ~ Isaiah 30:26 NLT

"I will give you back your health and heal your wounds," says
the LORD [Jehovah-Rophe]. "For you are called an outcast—
'Jerusalem for whom no one cares.'" ~ Jeremiah 30:17 NLT

Jehovah-Rophe Prayers

JEHOVAH-ROPHE HEALS

(Based on the promises found in Psalm 103)

_____ praises *Jehovah's* holy name with all that is within _____.

_____ remembers each of *Jehovah-Rophe's* benefits:

forgiveness of all _____'s sins and healing of all _____'s diseases.

Jehovah-Rophe has redeemed _____'s life from the pit,

crowning _____ with love and compassion,

and satisfying _____'s desires with good things

so that _____'s youth is renewed like the eagle.

_____ worships *Jehovah-Rophe*, who works

righteousness and justice for all the oppressed.

_____ is so thankful *Jehovah-Rophe* made

known his ways to Moses and the Israelites.

_____ knows that *Jehovah-Rophe* is

compassionate and gracious and is slow to anger,

abounding in steadfast love.

_____ is grateful that *Jehovah-Rophe* does not treat _____

as _____ deserves and

does not repay _____ according

to the punishment of _____'s sins.

_____ rejoices, for as high as the heavens are above the earth,

so great is *Jehovah-Rophe's* love for _____

and those who fear him.

As far as the east is from the west, that is how far *Jehovah-Rophe*

has removed _____'s rebellious acts from _____.

_____ rejoices over *Jehovah-Rophe*,

because _____ is washed clean and forgiven.

Amen.

✝

JEHOVAH-ROPHE RENEWS

(Based on the promises found in Psalm 103 and Philippians 4)

_____ rejoices as *Jehovah-Rophe* is _____'s Father and
has compassion for all his children.
_____ understands that *Jehovah-Rophe*
deeply loves _____ and those who fear him.
Jehovah formed _____ and
remembers that _____ and all his children are imperfect.
_____ is thankful that *Jehovah-Rophe* understands _____'s
frailty and limitations.
_____ trusts in *Jehovah-Rophe*, knowing that all human life is short-lived,
like a flower blossoming in the field, which loses its petals in the breeze, and
there is no longer any sign of it.
_____ is grateful for *Jehovah-Rophe's* mercy
from everlasting to everlasting toward _____.
_____ is grateful to *Jehovah-Rophe*, who renews _____'s
strength and blows fresh wind into _____.
_____ knows that _____ can do all things through *Jehovah-Jesus,*
who renews, strengthens, and undergirds _____
to do all the tasks that *Jehovah* calls _____ to do.
_____ praises *Jehovah* and all his work, for everywhere is his dominion.

Amen.
†

JEHOVAH-ROPHE REDEEMS

(Based on the promises found in Psalm 30)

_____ exalts *Jehovah-Rophe*, who lifted _____

out of the depths and did not let

_____ perish from the attacks from the enemy.

Jehovah-Rophe spared _____ from going down to the eternal pit.

_____ called on *Jehovah-Elohim* for help.

Jehovah-Rophe then brought _____ up from the grave and

breathed spiritual life back into _____.

_____ is one of *Jehovah-Rophe's* faithful children.

Jehovah-Rophe always takes care of his own, including _____.

_____ joyfully makes music and sings praises to *Jehovah-Rophe*.

_____ thanks *Jehovah* for his steadfastness to _____, who belongs to him.

_____ is grateful *Jehovah-Elohim's* anger lasts only a moment,

but his favor lasts a lifetime;

_____'s weeping may endure for the night,

but _____ rejoices in song in the morning.

_____ knows that he/she will never be shaken because

Jehovah-Rophe protects and redeems _____.

_____ is thankful *Jehovah-Rophe* pities _____.

Jehovah is _____'s helper!

Jehovah-Rophe has turned _____'s weeping into dancing.

Jehovah-Rophe has removed _____'s sadness and clothed _____ with joy.

_____'s soul praises *Jehovah-Rophe*, and _____ will not be silent.

_____ gives thanks to *Jehovah-Rophe* forever.

Amen.

†

JEHOVAH-ROPHE RESTORES

(Based on the promises found in Jeremiah 17, 30, and 33)

Jehovah-Rophe heals _____.

Jehovah-Rophe saves _____.

_____ praises *Jehovah-Rophe*.

_____ rejoices because he/she knows *Jehovah-Rophe* fights for him/her.

_____ will be nourished like a tree planted by the waters,

that spreads out its holy roots into the rivers of *Elohim*.

_____ does not fear the heat when it comes.

_____'s spiritual leaves will be continually green and moist.

_____ will not stop bearing fruit, nor be anxious or concerned

during a year of drought.

_____ knows that *Jehovah-Rophe* will devour all of _____'s enemies in

Jehovah-Rophe's perfect timing.

_____ knows that *Jehovah-Rophe* protects _____.

_____ exalts *Jehovah-Rophe*, who

restores and heals all of his/her wounds.

Blessed is _____, who trusts in *Jehovah-Rophe* alone.

_____ knows *Jehovah-Rophe* will bring

good health and healing to _____.

Because of *Jehovah-Rophe's* kindness and compassion,

_____ will enjoy abundant peace and security.

Amen.

†

JEHOVAH-ROPHE IS FAITHFUL

(Based on the promises found in Exodus 15
and 23; and Isaiah 41, 53, and 57)

Jehovah-Rophe is _____'s *Jehovah* who heals.

_____ exalts *Jehovah-Rophe*, who blesses _____ with food and water and

takes away all of _____'s illnesses.

_____ does not fear.

_____ rejoices that the great Healer, *Jehovah-Rophe,* is with _____.

_____ celebrates that *Jehovah-Rophe* strengthens, helps,

and upholds _____ with his righteous right hand.

_____ worships *Jehovah-Rophe*, who provides good health through

his mysterious, amazing, and eternal ways.

_____ stands firm on the promises of *Jehovah-Rophe's*

physical and eternal healing.

_____ rests in the knowledge that _____'s *Jehovah-Rophe*

guides and restores comfort to _____.

Jehovah-Rophe provides peace and healing to _____ and those far and near.

_____ knows that *Jehovah-Jesus* was despised and rejected by humanity,

a man of suffering, and familiar with pain.

_____ is humbled that Jesus was willingly pierced and

crushed for _____'s transgressions.

_____ is in awe that *Jehovah-Jesus* took up _____'s suffering.

_____ is grateful to *Jehovah-Jesus* for receiving

the punishment that brought _____ peace.

Jesus Christ's wounds, therefore, heal _____.

Amen.

†

JEHOVAH-ROPHE IS MERCIFUL

(Based on the promises found in Jeremiah 33; James 5; and 1 Peter 5)

_____ knows it is *Jehovah-Rophe* who brings health and healing to _____.
Jehovah-Rophe blesses _____ with an abundance of peace and truth.
_____ praises *Jehovah-Rophe*, who cleanses and
pardons _____ from all of his/her sins.
_____ knows that *Jehovah-Rophe* is a name of joy, praise,
and honor before all nations of the earth. All shall hear all the
good that *Jehovah-Rophe* does throughout the world.
_____ does not tremble in fear, for *Jehovah-Rophe* covers _____.
_____ casts out all of his/her anxieties on *Jehovah-Rophe*.
_____ welcomes the humbling through the mighty hand of *Jehovah-Rophe*,
so that at the proper time, *Jehovah-Rophe* will exalt _____.
_____ is sober-minded and watchful, acknowledging that _____'s adversary,
the devil, prowls around like a roaring lion, seeking someone to devour.
_____ resists the enemy by standing firm in faith,
understanding that believers throughout the world
are also experiencing the same kind of temptation.
_____ has comfort in the knowledge that after
_____ has suffered for a little while,
Jehovah-Rophe will restore, confirm, strengthen, and establish _____.
_____ confesses his/her sins to other believers,
for _____ knows that the prayer of a righteous person is powerful and effective.
_____ knows that prayers offered in faith to *Jehovah-Rophe* for healing
are subject to *Jehovah-Rophe's* divine will and
the sick person will be made well in this life or eternity.
_____ praises *Jehovah-Rophe,* who has dominion
over all things, forever and ever.

Amen.

†

JEHOVAH-ROPHE, THE LIVING WATERS

_____ knows that *Jehovah-Rophe* heals and redeems.

_____ is grateful that *Jehovah-Rophe* first revealed his miraculous healing name to the millions of Israelites who fled the oppression of slavery in Egypt.

Jehovah-Rophe provides living waters for _____.

_____ rejoices because the *Elohim* who inexplicably parted the Red Sea and drowned the enemies of the Israelites is the same *Jehovah* who protects, provides, and heals _____.

_____ rejoices that *Jehovah-Rophe* allowed his Son, *Jehovah-Jesus,* to be placed in the bitter waters of sin, permitting access to the sweet, drinkable, and thirst-quenching springs of *Jehovah-Rophe.*

_____ worships *Jehovah-Jesus*, who became sin for _____ and took the punishment for all _____'s sins on the cross.

_____ knows that all who believe in Jesus Christ as Lord, Savior, and *Jehovah-Jesus* will have eternal life.

_____ has peace because *Jehovah-Rophe* not only heals _____ from his/her physical ailments, but he also rescues, heals, and redeems _____ from his/her greatest disease—sin.

_____ rejoices in the confirmation that *Jehovah-Jesus* has removed the eternal consequences of _____'s sin, misery, and death.

_____ affirms the covering of *Jehovah-Jesus's* living waters that boldly declare _____'s spiritual reconciliation with *Jehovah-Elohim.*

Amen.

✝

My Prayers to Jehovah-Rophe

See, I am the only **Elohim**. There are no others.
I kill, and I make alive. I wound, and I heal,
and no one can rescue you from my power. ~ Deuteronomy 32:39

REMEMBERING HOW MUCH our *Jehovah-Rophe* delights in hearing and answering our prayers before praying them provides us great reassurance. Also, we can receive comfort that our great *Jehovah-Rophe* is our Healer, which means someone or something that cures diseases or heals injuries by means other than conventional medical treatment, person or thing that mends or repairs something, or something that alleviates distress or anguish.[35]

1. How does knowing that *Jehovah-Rophe* is our great and divine Healer change your prayer requests?

   _____

   _____

   _____

   _____

2. What would be your response if *Jehovah-Rophe* decides not to heal you or your loved one on this side of eternity?

   _____

   _____

3. How does the knowledge of our amazing *Jehovah-Rophe*, who loves you as much as his own Son and will not withhold any good gift from you, alter your prayer request?

4. How does praying to your *Jehovah-Rophe*, who always redeems, renews, and restores his servants for the task he calls us to beforehand, encourage you?

5. List your prayer requests to your *Jehovah-Rophe*, your Healer and Redeemer, who will never leave nor forsake you:

"Are you in sorrow? Prayer can make your affliction sweet and strengthening. Are you in gladness? Prayer can add to your joy a celestial perfume. Are you in extreme danger from outward or inward enemies? Prayer can set at your right hand an angel whose touch could shatter a millstone into smaller dust than the flour it grinds, and whose glance could lay an army low. What will prayer do for you? I answer: All that God can do for you. 'Ask what I shall give thee.'"[36]

~ Farrar

~ 7 ~

JEHOVAH-NISSI

יְהֹוָה נִסִּי

/Je-ho'vah Nis-see/

Jehovah-Nissi Meaning

THE LORD IS MY BANNER | GOD OF MIRACLES

MOSES ERECTED AN altar in response to the Israelites' first battle and victory over the Amalekites after leaving the bondage of slavery in Egypt. He called it *Jehovah-Nissi,* which means "the Lord is my banner." During biblical times, a banner wasn't a fabric flag, but rather a bare signal pole, ensign, or standard with a bright shining ornament that sparkled in the sun—for the Hebrew word for banner means "to glisten." Among the Jews, *nissi* is also interchangeable with the word *miracle.*[37]

This initial clash transformed the Israelites into warriors and confirmed who fought for them—the all-powerful *Elohim.* The Israelites dominated as long as Moses held up his *Elohim*-given staff of miracles throughout the battle. Israel's enemies prevailed when he became weary and lowered his arms and staff. Moses's brother Aaron and Hur (Aaron's chief assistant and priest) placed a large rock for Moses to sit on. Each man then held up one of Moses's arms until Joshua, the leader of this motley crew of ex-slaves, defeated the well-trained Amalekite army.

This conflict established to the Israelites that their *Jehovah* was not only their provider and LORD but also their protector. Moses's rod emulated the bright countenance of their *Jehovah,* who ensured victory for his people. As Christians, the cross of Christ is our banner throughout our spiritual warfare. The name *Jehovah-Nissi* points to our *Jehovah-Jesus,* as we go from strength to strength in our victories.[38]

Jehovah-Nissi Scripture

The Amalekites fought Israel at Rephidim. Moses said to Joshua, "Choose some of our men. Then fight the Amalekites. Tomorrow I will stand on top of the hill. I will hold in my hand the staff *Elohim* told me to take along." Joshua did as Moses told him and fought the Amalekites, while Moses, Aaron, and Hur went to the top of the hill. As long as Moses held up his hands, Israel would win, but as soon as he put his hands down, the Amalekites would start to win. Eventually, Moses' hands felt heavy. So Aaron and Hur took a rock, put it under him, and he sat on it. Aaron held up one hand, and Hur held up the other. His hands remained steady until sunset. So Joshua defeated the Amalekite army in battle.

Yahweh [Jehovah] said to Moses, "Write this reminder on a scroll, and make sure that Joshua hears it, too: I will completely erase any memory of the Amalekites from the earth."

Moses built an altar and called it *Yahweh Nissi* [Jehovah-Nissi]. He said, "Because a hand was lifted against *Yah's* [Jehovah's] throne, *Yahweh* [Jehovah] will be at war against the Amalekites from one generation to the next." ~ Exodus 17:8–16

Thank God that he gives us the victory through our Lord *Yeshua* [Jehovah-Jesus] Christ. ~ 1 Corinthians 15:57

Jehovah-Nissi Prayers

JEHOVAH-NISSI IS MY ARMOR

(Based on the promises found in Ephesians 6)

_____ receives power from *Jehovah-Elohim* and his mighty strength.

_____ puts on all the armor that *Jehovah-Nissi* supplies so that

_____ can stand against the devil's strategies and schemes.

_____ knows this battle is not a wrestling match against a human opponent.

_____ is fighting against rulers, authorities, the powers who govern this

world of darkness, and spiritual forces that control evil in the heavenly world.

For this reason, _____ takes up all the armor that

Jehovah-Nissi so generously supplies.

_____ can then oppose the enemy during these evil days.

_____ will overcome all obstacles and stand his/her ground.

_____ is steadfast and immovable!

_____ fastens the truth around _____'s waist like a belt.

_____ puts on *Jehovah-Nissi's* breastplate of righteousness.

_____'s shoes are fitted with the readiness and firm

foundation to spread the gospel of peace.

_____'s faith is a shield to extinguish all the flaming arrows of the evil one.

_____ dons the helmet of salvation and takes up the

Word of *Elohim* as the sword of the Spirit.

_____ prays in the Spirit without ceasing in all situations

and with every kind of prayer and supplication.

To that end, _____ keeps alert with all perseverance, interceding

and making supplication for all of *Jehovah's* people.

Amen.

†

JEHOVAH-NISSI IS MY BANNER

(Based on the promises found in Psalm 60 and Isaiah 8)

Jehovah-Nissi's banner is raised over _____ and all who fear *Elohim*.

_____ and the saints of *Jehovah-Nissi* will

rally around his signal pole when attacked by the enemy.

_____ praises *Jehovah-Nissi* in advance for

his goodness, salvation, and mercy.

Jehovah-Nissi will rescue _____.

_____ stands on *Jehovah-Nissi's* faithful promises that he

alone will triumph and divide _____'s opponents.

_____ knows human assistance is worthless.

_____ will display great strength from *Jehovah-Nissi*.

The plans of _____'s enemies will never succeed

because *Jehovah-Nissi* is with _____.

_____ worships *Jehovah-Nissi* because he is holy and fights for _____.

Jehovah-Nissi is a safe place for _____ and a stumbling block

for all who comes against him.

_____ will wait for and hope in *Jehovah-Nissi* alone.

_____ praises *Jehovah-Nissi* in advance for the victory.

Amen.

†

JEHOVAH-NISSI PROTECTS

(Based on the promises found in Isaiah 30)

Jehovah-Nissi's banner is above _____ in the midst of his/her battles.

_____, standing up in faith up to his/her enemies,

rejoices as *Jehovah-Nissi* can cause one thousand people to flee.

Jehovah-Nissi will never leave nor forsake _____.

Jehovah-Nissi's banner blazes over _____.

_____ is grateful that *Jehovah-Nissi* is kind

and has compassion for _____.

_____ doesn't despair because _____ knows

Jehovah-Nissi hears his children when they appeal for help.

Jehovah-Nissi hears _____ as soon as he/she calls to him.

_____ has faith that *Jehovah-Nissi* will answer

_____ in his perfect timing.

_____ may face troubles and hardships, but

Jehovah-Nissi will soon rescue _____.

_____ will see *Jehovah-Nissi's* fortification with _____'s own eyes.

All of _____'s needs are provided for by *Jehovah-Nissi*.

Jehovah-Nissi's provisions are rich and nourishing.

_____ rests on the assurance that *Jehovah-Nissi* will command

armies of angels to cover _____ and

heal all of his/her wounds received in battle.

_____ praises *Jehovah-Nissi* for his protection,

watchfulness, and kindness over _____.

Amen.

†

JEHOVAH-NISSI IS JEHOVAH-JESUS

(Based on the promises found in Isaiah 11)

_____ is in awe of *Jehovah-Nissi*, who always provides an escape from trouble,
even when everything looks hopeless.

_____ rejoices that *Elohim* provided a shoot, our *Jehovah-Jesus*,
to come out from the stump of Jesse to bear amazing fruit.

_____ is grateful that the Spirt of *Jehovah* rested
upon *Jehovah-Jesus*, blessing him
with divine wisdom, understanding, power, and knowledge.

_____ trusts in *Jehovah-Jesus*, who judges righteously and
makes fair decisions for all his children, including _____.

_____ waits patiently for the second coming of *Jehovah-Jesus*, knowing
that the Messiah's kingdom will be filled with ultimate peace.

_____ is looking forward to experiencing that incredible harmony between
Jehovah and all of his Creation, as
wolves will live with lambs; leopards will lie down with
goats, calves, and lambs; and a little child will lead them.

_____ worships *Jehovah-Jesus* as the world will be filled
with the knowledge of *Jehovah*, like water covering the sea.

_____ knows that all the nations will come to *Jehovah-Jesus* and
bow down to him, and his resting place will be glorious.

_____ praises *Jehovah-Jesus* who stands as a banner, a
light upon a hill, and a glistening signal pole for the people
to gather around and see the great *Jehovah-Jesus*.

Amen.

✝

JEHOVAH-NISSI CARES

(Based on the promises found in Isaiah 49)

Just as a mother cannot forget her nursing child or baby in her womb,

Jehovah-Nissi will never neglect or ignore _____.

_____ rejoices in knowing that his/her name is inscribed on and

cut into the palms of *Jehovah-Nissi's* hands.

Jehovah-Nissi has surrounded _____

with other believers to undergird and help _____.

_____ delights in seeing *Jehovah-Nissi's* mighty hand at work.

_____ worships *Jehovah-Nissi* because of

his promises, protection, and banner over

_____ are steadfast and unchangeable.

Jehovah-Nissi declares over a grateful _____,

"Those who devoured you will be long gone.

I will lift my hand to signal the nations.

I will raise my flag for _____ and all my people.

Then you will know that I am *Jehovah-Nissi*.

Those who wait with hope for me will not be put to shame."

_____ praises *Jehovah-Nissi*.

Amen.

†

JEHOVAH-NISSI SAVES

(Based on the promises found in Numbers 21; John 3; and Hebrews 12)

_____ knows that *Jehovah-Nissi* disciplines
those he loves and accepts as his children.
Jehovah's correction is a clear indication that
_____ is one of his children and
not an illegitimate child without a father.
_____ quickly repents of any offensive ways and
does not repeat the sin.
Like the Israelites who needed to lift their gaze to
Moses's signal pole with a bronze snake on it to be healed,
_____ looks to *Jehovah-Jesus*, to be reconciled with *Elohim*
and have eternal life.
_____ rejoices that *Elohim*
sent his only Son into the world,
not to punish the world, but to save the world.
_____ knows those who trust in *Jehovah-Jesus* won't be condemned.
_____ is saddened and prays for those who
don't believe in *Elohim's* only Son,
Jehovah-Jesus, and are doomed to spend eternity in hell.
_____ praises *Jehovah-Nissi* for sending his only Son as a signal pole
and a reminder to lift our gazes to
Jehovah-Jesus, our Lord and Savior.

Amen.

†

JEHOVAH-NISSI RULES

(Based on the promises found in Genesis 18; Job 42; Luke
1 and 18; Mark 9 and 10; and Matthew 17 and 19)

_____ boldly declares, "*Jehovah-Nissi*, I know that you can do
anything, and no one can stop you. You are the Ruler over all things."
_____ praises *Jehovah* who reminded Abraham,
"Is anything too hard for *Jehovah*? I will return about this time next year,
and Sarah [at ninety years old] will have a son."
_____ understands why Mary questioned the angel Gabriel how she,
a young virgin, could conceive a child, especially the Son of *Elohim*.
_____ rejoices over Gabriel's response,
"For nothing will be impossible with God."
_____ also agrees with *Jehovah-Jesus* when he reminded his disciples,
"With man it is impossible, but not with *Jehovah*.
For all things are possible with *Elohim*."
And _____ agrees with *Jehovah-Jesus* when he told his
disciples that they only needed faith the size of the smallest
seed—a grain of mustard—to say to a mountain,
"Move from here to there."
_____ knows that if his/her prayer is in accordance with *Jehovah's* will,
the mountain will move—
for no request is too big for *Jehovah-Elohim*.
_____ worships *Jehovah-Jesus*, who encouraged his followers, like _____,
to step out in faith and pray big, bold prayers,
because nothing is impossible for *Jehovah-Nissi*.

Amen.
†

JEHOVAH-NISSI OF MIRACLES

_____ celebrates and agrees with Moses when he erected an altar and called it *Jehovah-Nissi* after the Israelites' first victory out of slavery.
_____ knows that during biblical times,
a banner wasn't a fabric flag,
but rather a bare signal pole, ensign, or
standard with a bright shining ornament that sparkled in the sun—
for the Hebrew word for banner means "to glisten."
_____ rejoices because the Hebrew word, *nissi,*
is interchangeable with the word *miracle.*
_____ knows *Jehovah-Nissi* is _____'s source of all amazing wonders.
_____ exalts the all-powerful *Elohim*, who fights for _____.
_____ declares that *Jehovah-Nissi* is _____'s provider and protector.
_____'s gaze is fixated on *Jehovah-Jesus's*
complete and saving work on the cross.
_____ knows his/her enemies will not prevail.
When _____ is weary,
Jehovah-Nissi will bring an "Aaron" and a "Hur"
to remind, help, and pray for _____.
_____ lifts his/her gaze to *Jehovah-Jesus*
and does not focus on the enemy.
_____ rejoices, as the cross of Christ
is _____'s banner for spiritual warfare as
_____ goes from strength to strength in victory.

Amen.
†

My Prayers to Jehovah-Nissi

But the Lord is faithful, and he will strengthen you and protect you from the evil one. We have confidence in the Lord that you are doing and will continue to do the things we command. May the Lord direct your hearts into God's love and Christ's perseverance. ~ 2 Thessalonians 3:3–5 NIV

A s WE CRY out in prayer to our Abba, which means Father or, more affectionately, "Papa" or "Daddy,"[39] allow yourself to dwell on the significance of *Jehovah-Nissi* as our Father who is also our defender.

1. As we focus on God as our protector, which means a person who keeps someone safe from harm or who is in charge of a kingdom,[40] how does knowing that our *Jehovah* is also our Guardian and King transform your prayer request?

_____

_____

_____

_____

_____

2. How does praying to your God and champion, *Jehovah-Nissi*, comfort you?

    _____
    _____
    _____
    _____

3. How does knowing that you are praying to *Jehovah-Nissi*, the God who delights in blessing you with miracles, transform your prayer requests?

    _____
    _____
    _____
    _____

4. Armed with the knowledge that *Jehovah-Nissi* already has the victory in your life, how does that truth alter your perspective of your trials?

    _____
    _____
    _____
    _____

5. Record your praises to your Father *Jehovah* or Abba before he answers your prayers, despite your situation:

    _____
    _____
    _____
    _____

"Wrestling prayer can wonders do,
Bring relief in deepest straits;
Prayer can force a passage through
Iron bars and brazen gates." ~ John Newton[41]

~ 8 ~

JEHOVAH-
M'KADDESH

/Je-ho'-vah M'-Kad'-desh/

Jehovah-M'Kaddesh

Meaning

THE GOD WHO SANCTIFIES

J EHOVAH-M'KADDESH MEANS "*JEHOVAH* who sanctifies." The Hebrew word for sanctifies means to dedicate, consecrate, and make holy, hallowed, or set apart. There is no other name that more accurately describes the character of *Jehovah* and his requirements of his people than the name *Jehovah-M'Kaddesh*— the God who sanctifies.[42]

Just as *Jehovah* sanctified the Sabbath and singled it out from other days as a day of rest, before the start of work (Genesis 1:24–2:3), the Holy One, *Jehovah*, is above everything in the universe and is set apart from all things. *Jehovah* is the first and the last, for there is no *Elohim* but him (Isaiah 44:6). His holiness is the vehicle for his beauty; it is the fundamental thing or core of God's character and his "awful purity."[43] It is the balance of all the attributes of *Elohim*.

Holiness gives *Jehovah* his grandeur and majesty, and more than anything else constitutes his fullness and perfection over us. And being the holy *Jehovah*, the antithesis of all evil, he demands holiness from his chosen people. *Jehovah*, in his omniscience, knows humanity and gives us the power to choose by our own free will but does not force us to be holy. But since our hearts are deceitful above all things and desperately wicked (Jeremiah 17:9), a cure is needed.

Jehovah-M'Kaddesh is the Holy One who graciously and mercifully sanctifies us as children of *Elohim*. And what *Jehovah-M'Kaddesh* was to his people in the Old Testament, the Lord Jesus Christ, our cure and *Jehovah-Jesus*, is to us in the New Testament.[44]

Jehovah-M'Kaddesh

Scripture

Yahweh [Jehovah] said to Moses, "Say to the Israelites, 'Be sure to observe my days of worship. This will be a sign between me and you for generations to come so that you will know that I am *Yahweh* [Jehovah-M'Kaddesh] who makes you holy.'" ~ Exodus 31:12–13

"Live holy lives. Be holy because I am *Yahweh* [Jehovah] your *Elohim*. Obey my laws, and live by them. I am *Yahweh* [Jehovah-M'Kaddesh] who sets you apart as holy." ~ Leviticus 20:7–8

"Be holy because you offer the food of your *Elohim*. Be holy because I, *Yahweh* [Jehovah-M'Kaddesh], am holy. I set you apart as holy." ~ Leviticus 21:8

"Never dishonor my holy name. I will show my holiness among the Israelites. I am *Yahweh* [Jehovah-M'Kaddesh], who sets you apart as holy." ~ Leviticus 22:32

Jehovah-M'Kaddesh

Prayers

JEHOVAH-M'KADDESH IS HOLY

(Based on the promises found in Genesis 2 and Exodus 19)

_____ rejoices that *Elohim* made heaven and earth and everything in them.

_____ is thankful that *Elohim* blessed the

seventh day and set it apart as holy

because on that day, *Elohim* stopped all his work of creation.

_____ is grateful that *Jehovah-M'Kaddesh* declared the Sabbath holy to give

_____ and all his saints a day of rest before each week starts.

_____ trusts in *Jehovah-M'Kaddesh* to equip

him/her to complete all _____'s work on the remaining six days of the week.

Jehovah-M'Kaddesh loves _____ enough to

set apart him/her for his holy service.

_____ knows that what *Jehovah-M'Kaddesh* consecrates is declared holy,

despite what man might say.

Jehovah-M'Kaddesh sanctifies _____ and

his people, for a reason—for service in his kingdom,

full-time ministry, or just to share *Jehovah-Jesus's* message of

hope to the people that *Jehovah* brings into his/her life.

_____ rejoices that *Jehovah-M'Kaddesh*

will never reject anyone he sanctifies.

_____ praises *Jehovah-M'Kaddesh*,

who through *Jehovah-Jesus's* complete work on the cross,

eternally washed _____ clean of all his/her sins.

Amen.

†

JEHOVAH-M'KADDESH IS RIGHTEOUS

(Based on the promises found in Isaiah 5 and 8; and Joel 2)

_____ worships *Jehovah-M'Kaddesh* who has done great things and will judge everyone on the earth who is living, has lived, and is to be born.

_____ rejoices that the one true *Elohim* shows himself holy and set apart as he always does what is right.

_____ comprehends the amazing, righteous, and sanctifying power of *Jehovah-M'Kaddesh*.

_____ fears the power of *Jehovah-M'Kaddesh* and knows that he is the only true source of protection for _____ .

_____ grieves that many will stumble, fall, and be broken, refusing the living knowledge, righteousness, and eternal life that comes from *Jehovah-M'Kaddesh*.

_____ will wait for *Jehovah-M'Kaddesh* and hopes only in him.

_____ knows that the day of *Jehovah-M'Kaddesh's* righteous judgment will come.

_____ intercedes in prayer for the unsaved to turn from their sins, accept *Jehovah-Jesus* as their Savior, and become a follower of the holy, one true *Jehovah-Elohim*.

_____ is not afraid of the days to come because he/she knows that *Jehovah-M'Kaddesh's* righteousness covers _____ .

_____ finds joy in *Jehovah-Elohim*.

_____ knows that *Jehovah-Jesus* is the one true Teacher of Righteousness.

_____ is grateful to *Jehovah* for choosing him/her as his child and placing his righteousness over _____ and his followers.

Amen.

†

JEHOVAH-M'KADDESH IS OUR JUDGE

(Based on the promises found in Isaiah 13 and 66)

_____ calls loudly to *Jehovah-M'Kaddesh*.

In prayer, _____ raises *Jehovah-Nissi's* banner on
the bare mountaintop of trials and suffering.

Jehovah-M'Kaddesh will assemble an army to
battle for _____ and his children.

Jehovah-M'Kaddesh will eventually come with the
weapons of fury to destroy the whole world.

_____ rejoices that the day of judgment from *Jehovah-M'Kaddesh* is near.

_____ understands that the destruction of the world by the
almighty *El-Shaddai* will come suddenly.

Every hand will hang limp, everyone's courage will fail, and all
will be terrified as pain and anguish seize them.

_____ knows that the wrath from the almighty *El-Shaddai* will destroy all
sinners who have not repented and trusted in *Jehovah-Jesus* as their Savior.

_____ is grateful for *Jehovah-M'Kaddesh's* righteousness
that covers _____ and all his saints.

Heaven is *Jehovah-M'Kaddesh's* throne and the earth is his footstool.

_____ is no longer under wrath but under grace due to
his/her trust in *Jehovah-Jesus* as his/her Savior.

_____ worships *Jehovah-M'Kaddesh* and knows that everything on earth and
the universe has come into being because he willed it to be so with just a word.

Jehovah-M'Kaddesh offers _____ peace like a river and
the wealth of the nations like an overflowing stream.

_____ is carried in *Jehovah's* arms and cuddled on his knees.

_____ rests in the assurance that *Jehovah-M'Kaddesh*
draws near and comforts _____.

Amen.

†

JEHOVAH-M'KADDESH SANCTIFIES

(Based on the promises found in Numbers 6 and Joshua 3)

Jehovah-M'Kaddesh sanctifies _____ and all his saints.

_____ knows that he/she is set apart by *Jehovah-M'Kaddesh*
like the Nazirites who vowed to abstain from drinking alcohol and vinegar,
eating grapes, and cutting their hair or going near a dead body.

_____ is grateful that *Jehovah-M'Kaddesh* considers _____ holy.

_____ is in awe of *Jehovah-M'Kaddesh*, who
makes _____ and his people righteous.

_____ knows that the *Jehovah-M'Kaddesh*
who consecrates his people before performing miracles,
like parting the Jordan River for the Israelites to cross,
is the same *Jehovah-M'Kaddesh* of today.

_____, like the Israelites, is astonished that *Jehovah-M'Kaddesh*
stopped the flowing Jordan River like a dam so the Israelites
could march across the dry, once-raging waters to accomplish
Jehovah-M'Kaddesh's will for the Israelites to enter their inheritance.

_____ knows there is no force of nature, demonic force, or
weapon, seen or unseen, that can deter *Jehovah-M'Kaddesh*
from fulfilling his promise to _____ and his children.
There is nothing beyond the hand, power, and might of *Jehovah-M'Kaddesh*.

_____ rejoices because *Jehovah-M'Kaddesh*
protects and cares for _____ and his children, whom he purifies for his glory.

Amen.

✝

JEHOVAH-M'KADDESH EQUIPS

(Based on the promises found in Jeremiah 1)

_____ declares the holiness of *Jehovah-M'Kaddesh* to everyone.

_____ rejoices that *Jehovah-M'Kaddesh* sanctifies

those he uses for his purposes.

_____ knows that for those *Jehovah-M'Kaddesh* foreknew,

he also predestined to be conformed to the image of his Son, *Jehovah-Jesus*.

_____ worships *Jehovah-M'Kaddesh*, who set apart

_____ for such a time as this, for this moment and this trial.

_____ exalts *Jehovah-M'Kaddesh*, who declares over _____,

"Before I formed you in the womb,

I knew you.

Before you were born,

I set you apart for my holy purpose."

_____ praises *Jehovah-M'Kaddesh*, who doesn't call the equipped

but equips the called, just like he did for Jeremiah.

For as *Jehovah-M'Kaddesh* told Jeremiah, he also proclaims over _____,

"You will go wherever I send you.

You will say whatever I command you to say.

Don't be afraid of people.

I am with you and I will rescue you."

_____ knows that the same *Jehovah-M'Kaddesh*

who put words into Jeremiah's mouth will help _____.

Jehovah will never renounce _____ and those he sets apart as holy.

_____ has peace knowing that *Jehovah-M'Kaddesh's*

righteousness covers _____ and all his saints.

Amen.

†

JEHOVAH-M'KADDESH IS TRUSTWORTHY

(Based on the promises found in James 1)

_____ worships *Jehovah-M'Kaddesh*, who sanctifies through trials.

Therefore, _____ counts it all joy when he/she meets trials of various kinds,

for _____ knows that the testing of _____'s faith produces steadfastness.

_____ allows steadfastness to have its full effect

so that _____ may be perfect and complete, lacking nothing.

If _____ lacks wisdom, _____ knows that he/she

must ask *Jehovah-M'Kaddesh*,

who gives generously to all without reproach, and _____ will receive.

_____ understands that he/she needs to ask in faith, without doubting,

for the one who doubts is like a wave of the sea driven and tossed by the wind.

_____ does not boast because _____ knows life

is like a vapor and will soon pass away.

_____ waits on *Jehovah-M'Kaddesh*.

_____ knows he/she is blessed and knows that

if he/she remains steadfast under trial,

he/she will receive the crown of life, which *Jehovah-M'Kaddesh*

has promised to those who love him.

_____ receives comfort that *Jehovah-M'Kaddesh*

cannot and does not tempt anyone with evil.

_____ rejoices as every good gift and every perfect gift

is from above, coming down from the Father of lights, with

whom there is no variation or shadow due to change.

_____ is quick to hear, slow to speak, slow to anger because _____ knows that

anyone who does not bridle their tongue, their faith is worthless.

_____ puts away all sin and receives salvation

with humility from *Jehovah-M'Kaddesh*.

Amen.

†

JEHOVAH-M'KADDESH IS HOLY

_____ knows that *Jehovah-M'Kaddesh* means the *Jehovah*
who sanctifies, dedicates, consecrates, and makes holy, hallowed, or set apart.
_____ rejoices that there is no other name that more accurately
describes the character of *Jehovah* and his requirements of his
people than *Jehovah-M'Kaddesh*—the God who sanctifies.
_____ worships *Jehovah*, who sanctified the Sabbath and
set it apart from other days as a day to rest.
_____ exalts the Holy One, *Jehovah-M'Kaddesh*,
who is set apart from and above all else in the universe.
_____ adores *Jehovah-M'Kaddesh* as the first and the last,
for _____ comprehends there is no *Elohim* but him.
_____ is in awe of *Jehovah-M'Kaddesh's* awful purity
and understands that this name is the very core of *Jehovah's*
character and the balance of all the attributes of *Elohim*.
_____ acknowledges that *Jehovah-M'Kaddesh's* holiness gives
Jehovah his grandeur and majesty while constituting his fullness and perfection.
_____ gives all the glory to *Jehovah-M'Kaddesh*,
who is the antithesis of all evil,
knowing that he demands righteousness from _____ and his chosen people.
_____ is comforted as *Jehovah*, in his omniscience, knows him/her and
gives him/her the power to choose with his/her free
will, but does not force _____ to be holy.
_____ and all *Jehovah-M'Kaddesh's* people recognize that the
human heart is deceitful above all things and desperately wicked.
_____ rejoices that a cure for _____'s sin is
provided in *Jehovah-M'Kaddesh*.
_____ praises both the *Jehovah-M'Kaddesh* in the Old Testament and
the *Jehovah-Jesus* in the New Testament because they are one and the same.

Amen.

†

My Prayers to Jehovah-M'Kaddesh

"But God." ~ Acts 13:30 ESV

BEFORE WE CRY out in prayer to our *Jehovah-M'Kaddesh*, our LORD who sanctifies us and cleanses us from all our sin, allow yourself to rest in his purity that completely covers us, making us righteous.

1. As we focus on *Jehovah-M'Kaddesh* as our sanctifier, which means someone who sets us apart for a sacred purpose and frees us from our sin,[45] how does knowing that we are now holy like *Jehovah* transform your prayer request?

   ....

   ....

   ....

   ....

2. Does knowing you are praying to your *Jehovah-Jesus*, who loves you enough to die for your sanctification, comfort you? Why or why not?

   ....

   ....

   ....

   ....

3. How does the knowledge that you are pronounced righteous and not under condemnation by Jehovah-M'Kaddesh change your prayer requests?

-----

4. List your prayer requests to our *Jehovah-M'Kaddesh,* who graciously gives us all things and does not spare his own Son to sanctify us (see Romans 8:32).

-----

5. Record your praises to your *Jehovah-M'Kaddesh* before he answers your prayers, despite your situation:

"Holiness… is the balance of all…the attributes of the Deity. Power without holiness would degenerate into cruelty; omniscience without holiness would become craft; justice without holiness would degenerate into revenge; and goodness without holiness would be passionate and intemperate fondness doing mischief rather than accomplishing good. It is this holiness that gives to God grandeur and majesty, and more than anything else constitutes His fullness and perfection."[46] ~ Nathan Stone

~ 9 ~

JEHOVAH-SHALOM
יְהֹוָה שָׁלוֹם

/Je-ho'-vah Shal-lom'/

Jehovah-Shalom Meaning

THE LORD IS PEACE

JEHOVAH-SHALOM SPEAKS PERFECT peace to our hearts and meets our greatest need—shalom with *Elohim*. Shalom is the product of fully being what we were created to be. It surpasses all understanding and sustains us through difficult times. In his own being, *Jehovah* is perfect peace and is the only source of reconciliation for all humanity. This name boldly declares, "I am *Jehovah* who sanctifies you and enables you to live in my presence and fellowship."[47]

Shalom in the Old Testament has been translated as whole, finished, restitution, and perfect. It also indicates harmony and reconciliation in a relationship based upon the payment of debt.[48] *Shalom* was and still is the most common greeting in the Bible and even in other lands. Jerusalem, the Messiah's city, means city of peace or possession of peace.[49] *Shalom* is most frequently translated as "peace" in its purest sense. It expresses the deepest desire and need of the human heart and the most significant measure of contentment and satisfaction in life.

This name directly points to our Savior, our "Prince of Peace." In this instance, the word is used as a "peace offering," which is the blood sacrifices of atonement on which reconciliation and peace were based.[50] *Jehovah-Jesus*, our ultimate shalom or "peace offering," restores our fellowship with *Elohim*, which was lost through the fall of man in the garden of Eden. This is the first word *Jehovah-Jesus* spoke to his disciples after rising from the dead, "Peace be with you."[51]

Thankfully, our shalom with *Elohim* is now possible through *Jehovah-Jesus*, who reconciled all humanity with *Elohim*.

Jehovah-Shalom Scripture

Yahweh [Jehovah] replied, "I will be with you. You
will defeat Midian as if it were only one man."
Gideon said to him, "If you find me acceptable, give me a sign
that it is really you speaking to me. Don't leave until I come
back. I want to bring my gift and set it in front of you."
"I will stay until you come back," he said.
Then Gideon went into his house and prepared a young goat and
unleavened bread made with quarts of flour. He put the meat in
a basket and the broth in a pot. Then he went out and presented
them to the Messenger of thE LORD under the oak tree.
The Messenger of *Yahweh* [Jehovah] told him, "Take the meat and
the unleavened bread, put them on this rock, and pour the broth
over them." Gideon did so. Then the Messenger of *Yahweh* [Jehovah]
touched the meat and the bread with the tip of the staff that was
in his hand. Fire flared up from the rock and burned the meat and
the bread. Then the Messenger of *Yahweh* [Jehovah] disappeared.
That's when Gideon realized that this had been the Messenger
of *Yahweh* [Jehovah]. So he said, "*Adonay Yahweh* [Adonai-Jehovah]!
I have seen the Messenger of *Yahweh* [Jehovah] face to face."
Yahweh [Jehovah] said to him, "Calm down! Don't be afraid. You
will not die." So Gideon built an altar there to *Yahweh* [Jehovah]. He
called it *Yahweh Shalom* [Jehovah-Shalom]. ~ Judges 6:16–24

Jehovah-Shalom Prayers

JEHOVAH-SHALOM IS PEACE

(Based on the promises found in Isaiah 66)

_____ knows that heaven is *Jehovah-Shalom's*

throne and the earth is his footstool.

_____ rejoices that *Jehovah-Shalom* has made

all these things in heaven and on earth.

_____ understands that *Jehovah-Shalom* is

the very reason why all these things have come into being.

Jehovah-Shalom pays attention to _____ and

those who are humble and sorry for their sins.

_____ trembles at his word and will see joy when

Jehovah-Shalom reveals his glory.

_____ worships *Jehovah-Shalom*, who offers shalom like a river and

wealth to the nations like an overflowing stream.

As a mother comforts her child, so will *Jehovah-Shalom* comfort _____.

Jehovah-Shalom will care for, feed, and cuddle _____ in his arms.

_____ will flourish as bountiful as new grass.

The power of *Jehovah-Shalom* will be made known to _____, his servant.

Jehovah-Shalom will come with fire and with his chariots

like a thunderstorm to condemn his enemies.

Jehovah-Shalom will pay back his adversaries with

burning anger, and punish them with flames.

Jehovah-Shalom will judge all people of the earth with his sword and fire.

_____ has shalom because of *Jehovah-Jesus's* complete work on the cross.

Amen.

✝

JEHOVAH-SHALOM'S PROMISES

(Based on the promises found in Numbers 6; Leviticus 26; Isaiah 32;
Luke 1 and 2; Colossians 3; and Romans 8 and 15)

_____ knows that sin's corrupt nature and attitude lead to death,
but a spiritual disposition steeped in *Jehovah-Shalom* leads to life.

Jehovah-Shalom gives light to _____.

Jehovah-Shalom covers _____ with peace, calmness, and safety.

_____ praises *Jehovah-Shalom*, who is loving and
merciful, and brings each day into being.

Jehovah-Shalom's peace flows freely to _____, who is bathed in his shalom!

_____ understands *Jehovah-Shalom's* promises.

_____ lives by *Jehovah's* laws and carefully obeys his commands.

Jehovah-Shalom provides for _____ at the right time, and he/she is fruitful.

_____ will eat abundantly and live securely in the land.

Whoever _____ uses *Jehovah's* name to bless, they will be blessed.

Jehovah-Shalom is with _____, and his peace blankets _____.

Jehovah-Shalom has called _____ into his
peace, and he/she is beyond thankful.

Jehovah-Shalom reigns in _____'s life.

Jehovah-Shalom guides _____ into the way of peace.

Jehovah-Shalom will bring peace to _____, and no one will terrify _____.

Jehovah-Shalom blesses and watches over _____.

Jehovah-Shalom smiles over and is kind to _____.

Jehovah-Shalom will look on _____ with favor and give _____ peace.

_____ exalts *Jehovah-Shalom*.

Amen.

✝

JEHOVAH-SHALOM IS REST

(Based on the promises found in John 14 and 16)

Jehovah-Jesus gives _____ an everlasting sense of shalom and
doesn't give the kind of peace that the world gives.

_____ is not troubled or afraid.

Jehovah-Jesus's shalom is with _____ even
though he/she experiences hardships.

_____ lifts his/her gaze to *Jehovah-Shalom* because
Jehovah-Jesus has overcome the world.

_____ rejoices that *Jehovah-Jesus* offers his shalom
to _____ and all who follow him.

_____ joyfully comes to *Jehovah-Jesus* and learns
from him because he is gentle and humble.

_____ finds rest in *Jehovah-Jesus* because his
yoke is easy and his burden is light.

_____ continues to love others.

_____ shows hospitality because he/she might unknowingly
be showing generosity to angels. _____ remembers those
in prison as if he/she was incarcerated with them.

_____ identifies with those who are mistreated
as if he/she was being abused.

_____ honors the sanctity of marriage and
encourages husbands and wives to be faithful to each other.

_____ understands that *Jehovah-M'Kaddesh* will judge everyone.

_____ prays for all to repent and turn from their depravities.

Jehovah-Shalom will never abandon or leave _____.

Jehovah-Shalom helps _____, and he/she is not afraid.

_____ worships *Jehovah-Shalom*, who is the
same yesterday, today, and forever.

Amen.

✝

JEHOVAH-SHALOM RESTORES

(Based on the promises found in Isaiah 26)

_____ rejoices that *Jehovah-Shalom* keeps _____ in perfect peace.

_____ trusts in *Jehovah-Shalom* alone.

_____'s thoughts are fixed on *Jehovah-Shalom*!

_____ worships *Jehovah-Elohim*, who is _____'s eternal Rock.

_____ understands that *Jehovah-Elohim* humbles

the proud and brings down the arrogant.

_____ worships *Jehovah-Shalom*,

who does what is right and makes the path straight for _____.

_____ desires to glorify *Jehovah-Shalom*.

In the night, _____ searches for *Jehovah-Shalom*, and

in the morning, _____ earnestly seeks his shalom.

Jehovah-Shalom grants _____ peace.

_____ realizes that all he/she has accomplished is from *Jehovah*.

_____ worships *Jehovah-Shalom* and gives him all the glory!

In distress, _____ searches for *Jehovah-Shalom* and

prays for his wise discipline for grace, strength, and joy.

_____ knows that those who have faith in *Jehovah-Shalom* won't die;

instead, their bodies will rise again and they will have abundant life.

_____ rejoices with those who sleep in the earth and rise and sing for joy.

_____ understands that *Jehovah-Elohim's* life-giving

light will fall like dew on _____.

_____ cries out to *Jehovah-Shalom*—his peace pours over _____.

_____ worships *Jehovah-Shalom*, who alone provides eternal shalom.

Amen.

†

JEHOVAH-SHALOM IS LOVE

(Based on the promise found in 1 Corinthians 13 and 2 Corinthians 13)

_____ knows that if _____ speaks in the tongues
of men or angels, but does not have love,
_____ is only a resounding gong or a clanging cymbal.
If _____ has the gift of prophecy, fathoms all mysteries and knowledge,
and has faith to move mountains, but does not have love, _____ is nothing.
_____ understands that if he/she gives all his/her possessions to the poor, but
does not have love, _____ gains nothing.
_____ is patient. _____ is kind. _____ does not envy or boast.
_____ is not proud. _____ does not dishonor others.
_____ is not self-seeking. _____ is not easily
angered. _____ keeps no record of wrongs.
_____ does not delight in evil but rejoices with the truth.
_____ always protects, always trusts, always hopes, and always perseveres.
_____ never fails.
_____ knows that even prophecies will one day cease, tongues
will be eventually be stilled, and knowledge will ultimately
pass when _____ is with *Jehovah-Shalom* in eternity.
_____ trusts in *Jehovah-Shalom*, who provides all
things, including faith, hope, and love.
_____ discerns that the greatest of these gifts is love,
which is the best way to show others *Jehovah-Shalom*.
Jehovah-Shalom matures _____ in the faith.
_____ rejoices that he/she sees eternity as a reflection in a mirror.
_____ will one day see *Jehovah-Jesus* face-to-face.
Even though _____ presently knows *Jehovah-Shalom* only in part—
_____ rejoices that one day he/she will fully know *Jehovah-Shalom*.
_____ rejoices as the love and peace of *Jehovah-Shalom* is with _____.

Amen.

†

JEHOVAH-SHALOM IS MIGHTY

(Based on the promises found in 1 Chronicles 16 and Isaiah 9)

_____ gives thanks to the *Jehovah-Shalom* and
tells everyone about his mighty doings.
_____ sings praises to him, and _____ tells of his marvelous works.
_____ gives glory to and rejoices over *Jehovah-Shalom.*
_____ seeks the strength of *Jehovah-Shalom* and his face tirelessly.
_____ remembers *Jehovah-Shalom's* mighty
miracles and doesn't have spiritual amnesia.
_____ trusts in *Jehovah-Shalom's* authority,
which is seen throughout the earth.
_____ knows that all the people who walk in
darkness will see a bright light.
Jehovah-Shalom's will shine on those who live in the shadow of death.
_____ rejoices that *Jehovah-Shalom* has broken the yoke of sin
that burdens _____ and all humanity.
_____ worships *Jehovah-Shalom,* who expands the nations.
_____ is happy and content in *Jehovah-Shalom's* presence.
_____ rejoices over the promises that a child who was born
for us—the Son of *Jehovah-Elohim*—will save us.
_____ is grateful that *Jehovah-Elohim's* eternal government
of shalom and peace rests on *Jehovah-Jesus's* shoulders.
_____ praises *Jehovah-Jesus,* who is called Wonderful Counselor,
Mighty God, Everlasting Father, and *Sar Shalom,* or Prince of Peace.
_____ exalts *Jehovah-Jesus!*

Amen.

†

JEHOVAH-SHALOM IS PERFECT

_____ rejoices that *Jehovah-Shalom* speaks perfect peace to _____'s heart.

Thankfully, _____'s greatest need—shalom with *Elohim*—has been met.

_____ is grateful that *Jehovah* gives _____ shalom,

which is the product of fully being what _____ was created to be.

_____ knows that shalom surpasses all understanding

and sustains him/her through difficult times.

_____ worships *Jehovah*, who is perfect peace and

is the only source of peace for all humanity.

_____ rests in the knowledge that *Jehovah-Shalom's* name boldly declares,

"I am *Jehovah* who sanctifies _____ and enables _____

to live in my presence and fellowship."

_____ loves that shalom in the Old Testament is translated as

whole, finished, restitution, and perfect.

_____ is thankful to *Jehovah-Jesus* for the shalom that rests on _____,

which indicates harmony and reconciliation in a relationship

based upon the payment of debt.

Although shalom is most frequently translated as "peace," _____ knows in

its purest sense it expresses the deepest desire and need of _____'s heart.

_____ understands that shalom with *Jehovah* is the greatest

measure of contentment and satisfaction in _____'s life.

Jehovah-Shalom is _____'s Prince of Peace.

_____ rejoices in the faith that the title of *Jehovah-Jesus* means

a peace offering in which the blood sacrifices of atonement were

offered and reconciliation was achieved.

_____ knows that his/her ultimate shalom and fellowship with *Elohim*

has been restored through *Jehovah-Jesus*.

Amen.

✝

My Prayers to Jehovah-Shalom

A child will be born for us. A son will be given to us. The government will rest on his shoulders. He will be named: Wonderful Counselor, Mighty God, Everlasting Father, **Sar [Prince or Ruler of] Shalom**. ~ Isaiah 9:6

BEFORE WE CRY out in prayer to our great *Jehovah-Shalom*, our LORD who gives us peace that surpasses all understanding, let us first take a moment to comprehend that our greatest need of shalom with *Jehovah* has already been met. For shalom is the product of fully being what we were created to be.

1. As we focus on *Jehovah-Shalom*, who is perfect peace and is the only source of shalom for all humanity, how does knowing that we now possess *Jehovah's* peace that transcends all understanding transform your prayer request?

_____

_____

_____

_____

2. Does understanding that you are praying to *Jehovah-Shalom*, the only source of eternal peace, comfort you? Why or why not?

----

3. How does the knowledge that you have shalom with a holy and perfect God, the Creator of the Universe, your LORD and Master, and your Savior comfort you?

----

4. List your prayer requests to *Jehovah-Shalom*, who graciously covers you with his shalom, which far surpass any peace the world gives (see John 14:27).

----

5. Record your praises to your *Jehovah-Shalom*, the LORD of peace, before he answers your prayers, despite your situation:

"Prayer is not monologue, but dialogue. God's voice in response to mine is its most essential part."[52] ~ Andrew Murray

~ 10 ~

JEHOVAH-TSIDKENU

/Je-ho'-vah Tsid-kay'-noo/

Jehovah-Tsidkenu Meaning

THE LORD IS OUR RIGHTEOUSNESS

THE NAME *JEHOVAH-TSIDKENU* first appears when Jeremiah prophesied the fall, captivity, and restoration of Judah through the "righteous Branch." This "King" would reign, prosper, and execute judgment and justice throughout the earth[53] and would be called "*Jehovah* our righteousness" (Jeremiah 23:5–6).

The Hebrew word *tsidkenu* (righteousness) is derived from *tsedek* (to be stiff or straight), which cannot be accurately translated as there is no exact word to convey its full comprehension. We only see it exhibited clearly in *Jehovah's* character and actions. It signifies *Jehovah's* weighing of humanity by his scales of righteousness, justification, and acquittal.

Jehovah, who is perfectly righteous, cannot overlook our sin and lack of purity. Since punishment does not cleanse the sinner (see Romans 3:20; Jeremiah 17:9), a remedy for mankind is needed. The manifestation and provision of *Jehovah's* righteousness, which alone makes humanity acceptable to *Elohim*, was and is fully realized only in our *Jehovah-Jesus*.[54] For indeed, Christ died for sins once for all, the just and righteous for the unjust and unrighteous. He was and is one true innocent sacrifice for all the guilty, reconciling us with *Elohim* (1 Peter 3:18). What we are unable to do for ourselves, *Jehovah-Jesus*, as our *Jehovah-Tsidkenu*, did for us.

The name *Jehovah-Tsidkenu* reveals to us the method and measure of our acceptance before *Elohim*—cleansed by the blood of the Lamb and clothed in the white robe of *Jehovah*, our righteousness.

Jehovah-Tsidkenu Scripture

"The days are coming," declares *Yahweh* [**Jehovah**],
"when I will grow a righteous *Tsemach* [**Branch**] for David.
He will be a king who will rule wisely.
He will do what is fair and right in the land.
In his lifetime, Judah will be saved,
and Israel will live in safety.
This is the name that he will be given:
Yahweh Tsidqenu [**Jehovah-Tsidkenu**]."
~ Jeremiah 23:5–6

Jehovah-Tsidkenu Prayers

JEHOVAH-TSIDKENU RESTORES

(Based on the promises found in 2 Chronicles 7; Romans 8; Isaiah 38; and Jeremiah 29)

_____, who is called by name, will become humble

and seek the face of *Jehovah-Tsidkenu*.

When _____ turns from all wickedness and

calls upon *Jehovah-Tsidkenu* in prayer,

Jehovah-Tsidkenu will hear _____ from heaven.

_____ knows it was *Jehovah-Tsidkenu's* love that

rescued _____ from the pit of destruction.

_____ knows deep in his/her heart, he/she is

completely forgiven from all of his/her sins.

Jehovah-Tsidkenu listens to _____ and hears his/her prayers.

_____ praises *Jehovah-Tsidkenu*, who restores _____'s health.

_____ understands that all suffering he/she had to

endure is for _____'s benefit because

Jehovah-Tsidkenu works ALL things for good.

_____ worships *Jehovah-Tsidkenu*, who is gracious and merciful to _____.

_____'s hope is only in *Jehovah-Tsidkenu*.

Jehovah-Tsidkenu is _____'s strength every morning and before he/she goes

to bed at night. *Jehovah-Tsidkenu* is _____'s salvation in times of trouble.

Jehovah-Tsidkenu knows the plans he has for _____,

plans to prosper _____ and not to harm _____.

Jehovah-Tsidkenu has plans of hope and a future for _____.

With all of _____'s heart, _____ seeks and finds *Jehovah-Tsidkenu*.

_____ is declared righteous and restored by *Jehovah-Tsidkenu*.

Amen.

†

JEHOVAH-TSIDKENU IS MY RIGHTEOUSNESS

(Based on the promises found in Isaiah 54)

_____ rejoices that *Jehovah-Tsidkenu*'s eternal

covenant of peace is with _____.

Jehovah-Tsidkenu will enlarge _____'s territory

and will expand _____'s tent.

In obedience, _____ stretches out the curtains of his/her dwelling place

and strengthens the foundations.

_____ does not fear and is not ashamed, nor is he/she

discouraged and disgraced.

_____ knows *Jehovah-Tsidkenu* covers _____.

_____ forgets the shame of his/her youth, as *Jehovah-Tsidkenu*

no longer condemns or remembers _____'s sins.

_____ exalts *Jehovah-Tsidkenu* as _____'s

Redeemer—the *Elohim* of the whole earth.

Jehovah-Elohim has called _____, who once

was rejected and grieved in spirit.

_____ trusts in *Jehovah-Tsidkenu* even though it might have felt like

Jehovah-Tsidkenu deserted _____ in the midst of his/her suffering.

Jehovah-Tsidkenu gathers _____ in his loving arms

with an everlasting love and great compassion.

_____ worships *Jehovah-Tsidkenu*, who is no longer angry with _____

because of the blood of *Jehovah-Jesus* that covers _____.

_____ knows that the mountains may leave and the hills may be removed,

but *Jehovah-Tsidkenu's* steadfast love shall not depart from _____.

Jehovah-Tsidkenu's covenant of peace shall not be removed from _____.

_____ praises *Jehovah-Tsidkenu*, who is _____'s righteousness.

Amen.

✝

JEHOVAH-TSIDKENU PROTECTS

(Based on the promises found in Isaiah 54)

Even though _____ may feel afflicted, stormed-tossed, and not comforted,

_____ rejoices because *Jehovah-Tsidkenu* will rebuild

_____ with precious stones and will set his/her foundations with sapphires.

Jehovah-Tsidkenu will rebuild _____'s towers with rubies,

gates with sparkling stones, and walls with precious stones.

_____ praises *Jehovah-Tsidkenu* for his promise that all _____'s

children will be taught by *Jehovah-Tsidkenu* and have eternal peace.

_____ will be honored and established with integrity by *Jehovah-Tsidkenu*.

_____ will be far from oppression and destruction.

_____ will not be afraid.

If anyone attacks _____, it will not be from *Jehovah-Tsidkenu*, and

whoever assaults him/her will be defeated.

_____ worships *Jehovah-Tsidkenu*, who has created blacksmiths

to produce useful tools to destroy the wicked.

_____ stands on *Jehovah-Tsidkenu's* promises

that no weapon fashioned against _____ will succeed.

Jehovah-Tsidkenu will provide an answer for _____

for anyone who accuses him/her.

_____ rests in the assurance of *Jehovah-Tsidkenu's* protection,

which is bestowed upon all his servants.

_____'s victory comes from *Jehovah-Tsidkenu*.

_____ has peace knowing that he/she is declared

righteous by *Jehovah-Tsidkenu*.

Amen.

†

JEHOVAH-TSIDKENU IS MY JUDGE

(Based on the promises found in Psalm 7)

_____ takes refuge only in *Jehovah-Tsidkenu*.

_____ calls out to *Jehovah-Tsidkenu*, who saves and rescues _____.

_____ boldly declares *Jehovah-Tsidkenu* is his/her *Elohim*.

_____ rests on the assurance that *Jehovah-Tsidkenu* will arise in anger and

defend _____ against the fury of his/her attackers.

_____ knows that an assembly of people will

gather around *Jehovah-Tsidkenu*,

who judges all the people of the world.

_____ implores *Jehovah-Tsidkenu* to thwart the plans of the enemy and

bring the efforts of sinful people to an end.

_____ knows that *Jehovah-Tsidkenu* examines thoughts and emotions of

every human being who was, is, and will be.

_____'s shield is the one and only *Jehovah-Tsidkenu*.

Jehovah-Tsidkenu is _____'s judge and is angered by injustice every day.

_____ knows that it is only by the grace of

Jehovah-Tsidkenu that a person can change.

_____ intercedes daily and prays for _____'s enemies.

_____ gives thanks to *Jehovah-Tsidkenu* for his righteousness.

_____ praises the name of *Jehovah-Tsidkenu*,

the holiest being who was, is, and ever will be.

Amen.

✝

JEHOVAH-TSIDKENU FIGHTS FOR HIS PEOPLE

(Based on the promises found in Psalm 9)

_____ thanks *Jehovah-Tsidkenu* with his/her entire heart.

_____ will joyfully tell about all the miracles *Jehovah-Tsidkenu* has done in _____'s life.

_____ makes music and praises *Jehovah-Tsidkenu's* name.

_____ knows *Jehovah-Tsidkenu* will make his/her enemies retreat at the perfect time.

The wicked stumble and vanish in the holy presence of *Jehovah-Tsidkenu*.

_____ rejoices as *Jehovah-Tsidkenu* has defended his/her righteousness.

_____ worships *Jehovah-Tsidkenu*, who already has the victory over his/her eternal enemy.

The battle of Satan is finished—his kingdom is in ruins for eternity.

_____ adores *Jehovah-Tsidkenu*, who is enthroned forever.

Jehovah-Tsidkenu alone judges everyone on the earth fairly.

Jehovah-Tsidkenu is _____'s stronghold in times of trouble.

_____ trusts in the name *Jehovah-Tsidkenu*.

_____ praises *Jehovah-Tsidkenu*, who has never deserted _____.

_____ implores *Jehovah-Tsidkenu* to arise and not let the wicked prosper or gain power.

_____ rejoices because *Jehovah-Tsidkenu* passes judgment over all the nations.

_____ knows that *Jehovah-Tsidkenu's* rulings are righteous and, therefore, good.

Amen.

†

JEHOVAH-TSIDKENU IS KING

(Based on the promises found in Psalm 97)

_____ exalts *Jehovah-Tsidkenu* as the holy, blameless, and eternal King.

_____ is in awe as clouds and darkness surround *Jehovah-Tsidkenu* while
righteousness and justice are the foundations of his throne.

_____ knows that an all-consuming fire spreads
ahead of *Jehovah-Tsidkenu* and that

_____ is covered and protected by the blood of *Jehovah-Jesus.*

This holy and righteous blaze burns *Jehovah-Tsidkenu*'s enemies, and
his flashes of lightning light up the entire world.

_____ stands in faith and peace as the earth
sees the righteous wrath of *Jehovah-Tsidkenu* and trembles.

The mountains melt like wax in the presence of *Jehovah-Tsidkenu*, and
the heavens proclaim his righteousness.

All the people of the world see *Jehovah-Tsidkenu's* glory.

_____ knows that everyone who worships idols
will be put to shame as all the false gods bow to *Jehovah-Tsidkenu.*

_____ is delighted with *Jehovah-Tsidkenu's* judgments,
as he is above the whole earth.

_____ understands that those who love *Jehovah-Tsidkenu* hate evil.

Jehovah-Tsidkenu guards _____'s life and the lives of his children.

Jehovah-Tsidkenu alone rescues his servants, like

_____, from the power of evil people.

Jehovah-Tsidkenu's light dawns on _____.

_____ thanks *Jehovah-Tsidkenu* for his loving-kindness and mercy.

Amen.

†

JEHOVAH-TSIDKENU SANCTIFIES

_____ knows that the name *Jehovah-Tsidkenu* first appeared
when Jeremiah prophesied Judah's fall, captivity, and
subsequent restoration through the "righteous Branch."
_____ rejoices as *Jehovah-Tsidkenu* reigns, prospers, and
executes judgment and justice throughout the earth.
_____ understands the Hebrew word *tsidkenu* (righteousness)
is derived from *tsedek* (to be stiff or straight),
which cannot be accurately translated
as there is no exact word to convey its full understanding.
_____ sees this word exhibited clearly in *Jehovah's* character and actions.
_____ rejoices as the name *Jehovah-Tsidkenu* signifies *Jehovah's* weighing
of humanity by his scales of righteousness, justification, and acquittal.
_____ comprehends that since *Jehovah-Tsidkenu* is perfectly righteous,
he cannot overlook _____'s sin and lack of purity.
Since punishment does not cleanse the sinner,
_____ realizes that a remedy is needed.
_____ is in awe of the manifestation and provision
of *Jehovah-Tsidkenu's* righteousness,
which is only fully realized in our *Jehovah-Jesus.*
_____ worships *Jehovah-Jesus,* who died for _____'s sins once for all.
_____ has peace knowing that *Jehovah-Jesus* was and is one
true innocent sacrifice for all the guilty, including _____.
_____ understands that what he/she cannot do, *Jehovah-Jesus,*
as our *Jehovah-Tsidkenu,* did for _____ and all humanity.
_____ exalts *Jehovah-Tsidkenu* because his name reveals the irrevocable
method and measure of _____'s acceptance before *Elohim.*
_____ is cleansed by the blood of the Lamb and
clothed in the white robe of *Jehovah-Jesus.*

Amen.

✝

My Prayers to Jehovah-Tsidkenu

"The days are coming," declares *Yahweh* [**Jehovah**], "when I will keep the promise that I made to Israel and Judah. In those days and at that time, I will cause a righteous *Tsemach* [**Branch**] to spring up for David. He will do what is fair and right in the land. In those days Judah will be saved and Jerusalem will live securely. Jerusalem will be called *Yahweh Tsidqenu* [**Jehovah-Tsidkenu**]." ~ Jeremiah 33:14–16

BEFORE CRYING OUT in prayer to our *Jehovah-Tsidkenu*, our righteous LORD who blankets us with his purity, protection, and blamelessness, we need to take a moment to meditate on the power of forgiveness granted to us by *Jehovah-Jesus*. For we now are entirely washed clean and declared righteous all by the single act on the cross that reconciled us with our holy *Elohim*.

1. As we focus on *Jehovah-Tsidkenu* and his righteousness, which means the quality or state of being morally correct and justifiable, how does knowing that we are declared blameless by *Elohim* transform your prayer request?

    ....

    ....

    ....

    ....

    ....

2. How does the understanding that you are praying to *Jehovah-Tsidkenu*, your true source of eternal righteousness, console you?

3. How are you comforted with the knowledge that, due to your faith in Jehovah-Jesus's complete work on the cross, you, a sinner, are not found wanting on the scales of humanity but instead are declared righteous and therefore justified and acquitted by *Jehovah-Tsidkenu*?

4. List your prayer requests to our *Jehovah-Tsidkenu*, who graciously covers us with his holiness and purity:

5. Record your praises to *Jehovah-Tsidkenu*, your LORD of righteousness, before he answers your prayers, despite your situation:

"He who knows how to overcome with God in prayer has heaven and earth at his disposal." ~ Charles Spurgeon[55]

~ 11 ~

JEHOVAH-ROHI

יְהֹוָה רֹעִי

/Je-ho'-vah Ro'-ee/

Jehovah-Rohi Meaning

THE LORD IS MY SHEPHERD

*J*EHOVAH-*ROHI*, OR THE "LORD is my Shepherd," is first introduced in the Twenty-third Psalm and is by far the most precious designation of our *Jehovah*. No other name has brought more intimacy, comfort, or sweetness than this beautiful expression.[56] This Hebrew name in this Shepherd Psalm has formed the mold of faith from which countless saints have been poured.[57] The depth of *Jehovah's* amazing grace, care, and goodness are unfathomable without trials.

Metaphorically, *Rohi* indicates the relationship between a prince and his people, as well as a dear friend sharing the pleasures of life.[58] The primary meaning of *Rohi* is to feed or lead, as a shepherd does his flock. The intimacy shared between a shepherd and his animals is unique and touching to observe. The shepherd names each sheep, and they solely obey his voice and commands. By sleeping outside in open pastures with his flock, with his life the shepherd protects his sheep from those who would seek to destroy them. Therefore, the sheep fear no evil. Since the shepherd continually provides for the sheep's needs by leading them to green pastures to eat and still waters to drink, the sheep have no anxiety. Like the sheep, we are cared for, protected, and loved by our personal and great Shepherd.

Of all the names of God in the Old Testament, none is more perfectly personalized in the New Testament than *Jehovah-Rohi*. This name points to and is entirely fulfilled by the glorious Shepherd for us all, *Jehovah-Jesus*.

Jehovah-Rohi Scripture

Yahweh [Jehovah] is my *Roeh* [Rohi or Shepherd]. I am never in need. He makes me lie down in green pastures. He leads me beside peaceful waters. He renews my soul. He guides me along the paths of righteousness for the sake of his name. ~ Psalm 23:1–3

"'This is what *Adonay Yahweh* [Adonai-Jehovah] says: I will search for my sheep myself, and I will look after them. As a shepherd looks after his flock when he is with his scattered sheep, so I will look after my sheep. I will rescue them on a cloudy and gloomy day from every place where they have been scattered. . . . I will bring them out from the nations, gather them from the countries, and bring them to their own land. I will take care of my sheep and lead them to rest, declares *Adonay Yahweh* [Adonai-Jehovah]. I will look for those that are lost, bring back those that have strayed away, bandage those that are injured, and strengthen those that are sick.'" ~ Ezekiel 34:11–12, 15–16

Yeshua [Jesus] emphasized, "I can guarantee this truth: I am the gate for the sheep. All who came before I did were thieves or robbers. However, the sheep didn't respond to them. I am the gate. Those who enter the sheep pen through me will be saved. They will go in and out of the sheep pen and find food. A thief comes to steal, kill, and destroy. But I came so that my sheep will have life and so that they will have everything they need. I am the good shepherd. The good shepherd gives his life for the sheep. A hired hand isn't a shepherd and doesn't own the sheep. When he sees a wolf coming, he abandons the sheep and quickly runs away. So the wolf drags the sheep away and scatters the flock. The hired hand is concerned about what he's going to get paid and not about the sheep. I am the good shepherd. I know my sheep as the Father knows me. My sheep know me as I know the Father. So I give my life for my sheep." ~ John 10:7–15

Jehovah-Rohi Prayers

JEHOVAH-ROHI IS MY SHEPHERD

(Based on the promises found in Psalm 23)

_____ intimately knows his/her Shepherd, *Jehovah-Rohi*.

_____ lacks nothing.

Jehovah-Rohi makes _____ lie down in green pastures and leads him/her beside still waters.

Jehovah-Rohi refreshes _____'s soul.

_____ praises *Jehovah-Rohi* as he guides him/her along the right paths.

_____ knows *Jehovah-Rohi* does all of this because _____ is his and bears his name.

_____ understands that even though he/she walks through the darkest valley, _____ will fear no evil.

Jehovah-Rohi is with _____.

Jehovah-Rohi guides and defends _____ with his rod and staff.

_____ is comforted by *Jehovah-Rohi's* care and protection.

Jehovah-Rohi prepares a lavish banquet table before _____ in the presence of his/her enemies.

_____ is blessed, abundant with fullness, and his/her cup is overflowing.

Jehovah-Rohi exceedingly and abundantly provides for _____.

Jehovah-Rohi's goodness and love will follow _____ all the days of _____'s life.

_____ dwells in the house of *Jehovah-Rohi* forever.

Amen.

✝

JEHOVAH-ROHI IS MY REFUGE

(Based on the promises found in Psalm 43)

Jehovah-Rohi vindicates and defends _____'s
cause against any ungodly and evil people.
Jehovah-Rohi rescues _____ from the deceitful and unjust man.
_____ praises *Jehovah-Rohi* in advance as he delivers _____.
_____ takes refuge in *Jehovah-Rohi* when _____ is rejected.
_____ does not go about in mourning and sadness,
even amid the oppression of the enemy.
_____ worships *Jehovah-Rohi* as he sends out his
light and truth in protection and guidance.
Jehovah-Rohi leads _____ to his holy hill.
_____ has no fear because he/she dwells in the shelter of *Jehovah-Rohi*.
_____ celebrates *Jehovah-Rohi* and praises him with exceeding joy.
_____ sings worship songs and hymns to *Jehovah-Rohi*.
Jehovah-Rohi is always faithful.
_____ rebukes his/her soul when weary, discouraged, and forgetful
of *Jehovah-Rohi's* continual care, provision, and protection.
_____ lifts his/her gaze and hopes only in *Jehovah-Rohi*.
Jehovah-Rohi turns _____'s weeping into joy.
Jehovah-Rohi is _____'s salvation.

Amen.
†

JEHOVAH-ROHI'S TRANQUILITY

(Based on the promises found in Philippians 4)

_____ rejoices in *Jehovah-Rohi*.

_____'s gentleness is evident to all.

Jehovah-Rohi is inseparable from _____; he is always near _____.

_____ is not anxious about anything, but in

every situation, by prayer and petition,

with thanksgiving, _____ presents his/her requests to *Jehovah-Rohi*.

And the peace of *Jehovah-Rohi*, which transcends all understanding,

guards _____'s heart and mind in *Jehovah-Jesus*.

_____ focuses solely on whatever is true, whatever is noble, whatever

is right, whatever is pure, whatever is lovely, whatever is admirable.

If anything is excellent or praiseworthy, _____

concentrates only on such things.

_____ encourages his/her brothers and sisters in the faith to do the same.

_____ knows the importance of taking every thought

captive by arresting and throwing out all beliefs that do not

agree with *Jehovah-Rohi's* words and promises.

_____ worships *Jehovah-Rohi* as the shalom of *Jehovah*

excessively covers and abundantly fills _____.

_____ knows what it feels like to be in need.

_____ appreciates the times when he/she has plenty.

_____ has learned the secret of contentment in

any situation is to focus on *Jehovah-Rohi*.

Whether well fed or hungry, living in riches or want,

_____ rejoices over *Jehovah-Rohi*.

_____ can do all things through *Jehovah-Rohi*,

who gives _____ the strength and provisions he/she needs.

_____ knows that *Jehovah-Rohi* will meet all his/her desires

according to the riches of his glory in *Jehovah-Jesus*.

Amen.

†

JEHOVAH-ROHI IS FAITHFUL

(Based on the promises found in Psalm 33)

_____joyfully worships the faithful *Jehovah-Rohi*.

Jehovah-Rohi has put a new song on _____'s heart that he/she joyfully sings.

_____ knows that *Jehovah-Rohi's* words are

true and he is faithful in all he does.

_____ and the earth is full of *Jehovah-Rohi's* unfailing love.

_____ is in awe of the might and power of *Elohim*,

who created the heavens, stars, and the world by the breath of his mouth.

_____ rejoices that *El-Shaddai* can gather the waters of the

oceans, seas, and rivers into the palm of his hand.

Jehovah-Rohi foils the evil plans of the nations and

thwarts the wicked purposes of people.

_____ rests on the assurance that *Jehovah-Rohi* stands firm forever.

_____ understands that *Jehovah-Rohi* looks down from

heaven and sees all humanity because he has formed the

hearts of everyone and considers everything they do.

_____ knows that no king is saved by the size of his army and

no warrior escapes by his great strength.

Jehovah-Rohi's eyes are on _____.

_____ hopes in *Jehovah-Rohi's* unfailing love.

_____ waits patiently for *Jehovah-Rohi* to move at the perfect time,

for he is _____'s help and shield.

_____ knows that *Jehovah-Rohi* is faithful and his love is unfailing.

_____'s heart rejoices in *Jehovah-Rohi*.

_____ trusts *Jehovah-Rohi*.

Amen.

†

JEHOVAH-ROHI IS MY PROTECTOR

(Based on the promises found in Psalm 91)

_____ takes refuge in the shelter of *Jehovah-Rohi*.

Jehovah-Rohi is _____'s mighty fortress, whom he/she trusts.

Jehovah-Rohi rescues _____ from the snares of
his/her enemies and deadly plagues.

Jehovah-Rohi covers _____ with his feathers,
like a bird protecting its young.

_____ is sheltered under *Jehovah-Rohi's* great wings.

Jehovah-Rohi's faithfulness is like a shield around _____,
a rock-solid wall that protects him/her.

Because of *Jehovah-Rohi,* _____ does not
dread the terrors that haunt the night.

_____ stands against the attacks from the enemy during the day, evil
epidemics that lurk in the darkness, and disasters that wreak havoc at noon.

_____'s faith in *Jehovah-Rohi* is unwavering, even if a thousand
may fall on the left and ten thousand may die on the right.

Jehovah-Rohi commands his angels to guard _____.

_____ is safe in every way.

_____ rejoices as the hands of *Jehovah-Rohi's*
heavenly messengers uphold _____.

_____ will not crash, fall, or even graze his/her foot on a stone.

_____ safely tramples the lion and the serpent underfoot.

_____ rests on *Jehovah-Rohi's* promises.

Jehovah-Rohi rescues _____ from harm and
protects him/her from all danger.

Jehovah-Rohi knows _____ intimately by name.

Jehovah-Rohi will always be with _____.

_____ stands on *Jehovah-Rohi's* promises.

Amen.

†

JEHOVAH-ROHI IS MY RESTORER

(Based on the promises found in Psalm 37)

_____ is not preoccupied with evildoers.

_____ does not envy those who do wicked things.

_____ knows they will quickly dry up like grass
and wither away like dead plants.

_____ trusts in _Jehovah-Rohi_ to do good things.

_____ rejoices over _Jehovah-Rohi_.

Jehovah-Rohi gives _____ the desires of his/her heart.

Jehovah-Rohi acts on _____'s behalf.

_____ surrenders to _Jehovah-Rohi_ and trusts him.

_____ is able to release his/her anger and leave all rage behind because
he/she trusts in _Jehovah-Rohi_.

Jehovah-Rohi directs _____'s steps.

Jehovah-Rohi delights in _____.

When _____ falls, he/she will not be thrown down headfirst
because _Jehovah-Rohi_ holds on to his/her hand.

_____ has never seen a righteous person abandoned
or his descendants begging for food.

_____ avoids evil, does good, and lives forever in eternity because
_____ trusts in _Jehovah-Jesus_ for his/her salvation.

_____ rejoices that _Jehovah-Rohi_ will never abandon _____ and
will guard _____ forever.

Jehovah-Rohi is _____'s fortress in times of trouble.

_____ worships _Jehovah-Rohi_ as he rescues _____ from corrupt people.

_____ takes refuge in _Jehovah-Rohi_ alone.

Amen.

†

JEHOVAH-ROHI IS MY COMFORTER

(Based on the promises found in Isaiah 40)

_____, by *Jehovah-Rohi's* grace, comforts *Elohim's* children.

_____ knows *Jehovah-Jesus* is coming with power to rule with authority.

_____ rejoices as *Jehovah-Rohi* is _____'s
Shepherd who expertly cares for his flock.

_____ is at peace because *Jehovah-Rohi* gathers
_____ like a lamb in his arms.

_____ is in awe of *Jehovah-Rohi*, who stretches out the sky like a canopy and
spreads it out like a tent.

_____ humbly acknowledges that *Jehovah-Rohi*
has dominion over all the earth.

Jehovah-Rohi makes rulers unimportant and earthly judges worth nothing.

_____ knows that *Jehovah-Rohi* has no equal.

_____ has the assurance that the same power that *Jehovah-Rohi* used
to create the earth, universe, and every living thing, also protects _____.

Jehovah-Rohi gives strength to _____ and to those who grow tired.

Even though _____ may become weary,

_____ renews his/her hope in *Jehovah-Rohi*.

_____ will soar on wings like eagles.

_____ will run and will not become exhausted.

_____ will walk and not grow fatigued.

_____ worships *Jehovah-Rohi* as his/her Shepherd, King, and Refuge.

_____ rejoices that *Jehovah-Rohi's* words last forever and comfort _____.

Amen.

†

JEHOVAH-ROHI SUSTAINS ME

_____ knows that the Hebrew name of God
Jehovah-Rohi, or the "LORD is my Shepherd,"
is the most precious designation of *Jehovah*.
_____ rests in the assurance that the name *Jehovah-Rohi* has brought
more intimacy, comfort, and sweetness to _____ than any other name.
Jehovah-Rohi has formed the treasured mold of faith into which _____ and
countless saints have been poured.
_____ praises *Jehovah-Rohi* for his/her sufferings, for
_____ knows that the depth of *Jehovah's* amazing grace,
care, and goodness is unfathomable without trials.
_____ is comforted in the meaning of the word *Rohi,*
which indicates a relationship between a prince and his
people, a dear friend sharing the pleasures of life,
or a shepherd feeding or leading his flock.
_____ is reassured that the touching intimacy shared
between a shepherd and each of his animals is unique, just like
Jehovah-Rohi's relationship with each of his children.
Just as each sheep is named by the shepherd and they solely obey his voice
and commands, _____ follows *Jehovah-Rohi's* commands and voice.
_____ is thankful that that *Jehovah-Rohi* will never leave nor forsake
_____ and his children.
_____ rejoices that *Jehovah-Rohi* protects _____ when he/she is sleeping.
_____, like sheep with a good shepherd, fears no evil.
_____ has no anxiety, because his/her great
Jehovah-Rohi provides for _____.
_____ is cared for, protected, and loved by *Jehovah-Rohi.*
_____ delights in the name *Jehovah-Rohi,* because no name more personally or
more clearly points to *Jehovah-Jesus,* _____'s glorious Shepherd and Savior.

Amen.

†

My Prayers to Jehovah-Rohi

Christ carried our sins in his body on the cross so that freed from
our sins, we could live a life that has God's approval. His wounds
have healed you. You were like lost sheep. Now you have come back
to the shepherd and bishop of your lives. ~ 1 Peter 2:24–25

BEFORE WE CRY out in prayer to our *Jehovah-Rohi*, our eternal and
all-powerful Shepherd who faithfully provides, defends, and restores
us, let's first take a moment to meditate on the power of protection
over us by our *Jehovah-Rohi*, the Great Shepherd. Just as shepherds sleep with
and protect their sheep, our *Jehovah-Rohi* never slumbers. He keeps continual
vigilant watch over us, even when we are at our weakest.

1. As we focus on *Jehovah-Rohi* and his protection, which means a person
    or thing that prevents someone or something from suffering harm or
    injury, how does knowing that we are protected by the mightiest force in
    the known universe alter your prayer request?

    ----

2. Do you receive comfort in the understanding that you are praying to *Jehovah-Rohi*, who like any good shepherd, would lay down his life for you? And does the knowledge that *Jehovah-Jesus* has already done this for you on the cross give you peace? Why or why not?

3. List your prayer requests to our *Jehovah-Rohi*, who graciously covers you and cares for you with his indescribable power of restoration, peace, and provision:

4. Record your praises to your *Jehovah-Rohi*, your Great Shepherd, before he answers your prayers, despite your situation:

Psalm 91 is one of just a few places in Scripture that describe what we might call "guardian angels" (Exodus 23:20; Psalm 43:3). Though rare, these passages teach that God is not alone in maintaining and protecting His creation and His people. He has made a host of heavenly messengers ready to do His bidding, and His bidding is often to guard His people throughout their lives and protect them—sometimes from dangers they are not even aware of. ~ Notes from The Voice Translation on Psalm 91[59]

~ 12 ~

JEHOVAH-
SHAMMAH

/Je-ho'-vah Sham'-mah/

Jehovah-Shammah Meaning

THE LORD IS THERE

THE MEANING OF the name *Jehovah-Shammah* is "*Jehovah* is there." As each name reveals a deeper dimension and knowledge of God, this is the perfect name to climax our twelfth Old Testament revelation of the names of God. This name is the promise and pledge of the completion of the purpose of man's final rest—to glorify God and enjoy him forever.[60]

Jehovah-Shammah is found in the last verse of Ezekiel. The book of Ezekiel begins when Israel is at its lowest, both spiritually and as a nation. It ends with the final prophecy of Ezekiel, a Babylonian captive for twenty-five years. This closing message is one of hope and restoration for the land and the people to a state far beyond anything they had ever experienced in the past or could have imagined.[61] The pledge is found in the name *Jehovah-Shammah*, or "*Jehovah* is there."

The uniqueness of the people of Israel has always been the existence of *Elohim* dwelling in their midst. Unfortunately, in the Old Testament, *Jehovah's* presence (which was real and intimately felt by the Israelites) was conditional to the nation's obedience and faithfulness to follow *Jehovah's* commands.

Ezekiel didn't realize, nor did Israel, that this name and meaning points to and has been fully realized in the person of the *Jehovah-Jesus*. For when our King comes again in all his glory, we will finally see the full and physically amazing expression of *Jehovah-Shammah*. In the new heaven and earth, the dwelling of *Elohim* will be with men, and he will live with us. We will be his people, and *Jehovah-Elohim* himself will be with us (see Revelation 21:1–3).

Jehovah-Shammah Scripture

I saw the glory of the **Elohim** of Israel coming from the east.
His voice was like the sound of rushing water,
and the earth was shining because of his glory. . . .
Yahweh's glory came into the temple through the east gate.
The **Ruach** [**Holy Spirit**] lifted me and brought me into the inner courtyard.
I saw **Yahweh's** [**Jehovah's**] glory fill the temple. . . .
The city's name will *be:* **Yahweh** [**Jehovah**] **Shammah**.
~ Ezekiel 43:2, 4–5; 48:35

Jehovah-Shammah Prayers

JEHOVAH-SHAMMAH IS HERE

(Based on the promises found in Psalm 34)

_____ thanks *Jehovah-Shammah* and continually praises him.

_____ and those who are oppressed shall rejoice

when they hear the name *Jehovah-Shammah.*

_____ praises *Jehovah-Shammah's* greatness and goes to him for help.

Jehovah-Shammah will answer and rescue _____ from all his/her fears.

_____ is radiant when he/she looks to *Jehovah-Shammah.*

_____'s face will never be covered with shame.

Jehovah-Shammah's angels camp around and deliver _____.

_____ tastes and sees *Jehovah-Shammah's* goodness.

_____ takes refuge in *Jehovah-Shammah.*

_____ fears *Jehovah-Shammah* and is never in need.

_____ doesn't say evil or deceitful things as

_____ turns away from evil and does good.

_____ seeks peace and pursues it!

Jehovah-Shammah's eyes are on _____ and his righteous people.

Jehovah-Shammah hears _____'s cry for help.

Jehovah-Shammah rescues and protects _____ from all his/her troubles.

Jehovah-Shammah is near to _____ when his/her spirits are crushed.

_____ may experience many troubles, but he/she takes

refuge in *Jehovah-Shammah* and will never be condemned.

_____ praises *Jehovah-Shammah,*

who is always there and will never forsake _____.

Amen.

✝

JEHOVAH-SHAMMAH IS MY PROTECTION

(Based on the promises found in Psalm 121)

_____ looks up at the mountains and knows where his/her help comes.
_____'s rescue comes from *Jehovah-Shammah,*
the maker of heaven and earth.
_____ rejoices that *Jehovah-Shammah* will not let _____ fall.
Jehovah-Shammah continually watches over and cares for _____.
_____ praises *Jehovah-Shammah* as he guards his people, for
Jehovah-Shammah never rests or sleeps.
_____ stands firm in the knowledge that
Jehovah-Shammah is _____'s guardian.
_____ has peace that *Jehovah-Shammah* defends him/her.
Jehovah-Shammah is _____'s defense, especially
when man's protection fails.
_____ finds comfort in *Jehovah-Shammah* when difficulties arise.
_____ remains calm and sits under
Jehovah-Shammah's shade and security
during the most intense days or frightening nights.
_____ understands that *Jehovah-Shammah* guards
_____ physically, emotionally, and spiritually from every evil.
_____ praises *Jehovah-Shammah*, who preserves his/her life.
Jehovah-Shammah is _____'s protection
from this day and forever.

Amen.
†

JEHOVAH-SHAMMAH IS MY SUSTENANCE

(Based on the promised found in Psalm 63)

Jehovah-Shammah is _____'s sustenance.

At dawn, _____'s soul thirsts and searches for *Jehovah-Shammah*.

_____'s body longs for *Jehovah-Shammah* as in

a dry, parched land where there is no water.

_____ looks for *Jehovah-Shammah* to see his power and glory.

_____'s lips praise *Jehovah-Shammah* all day

because his mercy is better than life itself.

_____ thanks *Jehovah-Shammah* as long as he/she lives.

_____'s hands are lifted in prayers in the name of *Jehovah-Shammah*.

Jehovah-Shammah alone satisfies _____'s soul with the richest of foods.

_____'s mouth sings praises to *Jehovah-Shammah* with joyful lips.

_____ remembers *Jehovah-Shammah* as _____ lies in bed at night.

Through the dark, long nighttime hours,

_____ meditates on the goodness, care, and nearness of *Jehovah-Shammah*.

_____ worships *Jehovah-Shammah,* who alone is his/her help.

_____ sings joyfully in the shadow of *Jehovah-Shammah's* wings.

_____'s soul confidently clings to *Jehovah-Shammah*.

_____ is grateful as *Jehovah-Shammah's* right

hand supports and upholds him/her.

_____ trusts in *Jehovah-Shammah* as those who try to destroy

_____'s life will go into the depths of the earth.

_____ waits confidently for *Jehovah-Shammah* and

praises him in advance for his/her victory.

Amen.

†

JEHOVAH-SHAMMAH IS EVERYWHERE

(Based on the promises found in Isaiah 66; Psalm 139; and Isaiah 57)

_____ exalts how mighty *Jehovah-Shammah* is
and that no mere planet, temple, or person may contain him.
_____ rejoices that *Jehovah-Shammah* is always near him/her, even though
heaven is *Jehovah-Shammah's* throne and the earth is his footstool.
No house could be built to contain the great *Jehovah-Shammah.*
_____ worships *Jehovah-Shammah*, who is always there.
_____ knows there is nowhere anyone can hide from *Jehovah-Shammah.*
There is no place anyone can flee from *Jehovah-Shammah's* presence.
_____ rests in the understanding that
Jehovah-Shammah is everywhere,
from the heavens to the depths of the earth;
Jehovah-Shammah is ever-present.
Even if _____ had the wings of the dawn and
could soar the skies or
lived in the remotest part of the sea,
_____ would feel *Jehovah-Shammah's* presence.
_____ adores the high and exalted *Jehovah-Shammah,*
who lives forever and whose name is holy.
_____ comprehends that even though
Jehovah-Shammah dwells on a high and holy place,
he also resides with the downcast.
Jehovah-Shammah alone revives _____'s spirit and heart.

Amen.

✝

JEHOVAH-SHAMMAH AMONG US

(Based on the promises found in Exodus 23; Isaiah 7 and 9; John 1; Hebrews 1; 1 Corinthians 3 and 6; and Matthew 28)

_____ can feel the presence of *Jehovah-Shammah*.

_____ has deep peace in knowing that
Jehovah-Shammah's angels protect _____,
Jehovah-Shammah's presence goes with _____.
Jehovah-Shammah gives _____ rest.
_____ has the assurance that *Jehovah-Shammah* is fully with him/her.
_____ receives comfort in *Jehovah-Shammah's* ever-presence.
_____ rejoices that this was confirmed with a virgin
becoming pregnant and giving birth to a son named Immanuel,
meaning *Jehovah-Shammah*, or "God is with us."
_____ rejoices as this child is his/her Savior and is also called:
"Wonderful Counselor, Mighty God, Everlasting Father, and Prince of Shalom."
_____ knows that when *Jehovah-Jesus* was human and lived among
us, he was the physical representation of *Jehovah-Shammah*.
_____ worships *Jehovah-Shammah's* Son, who is the reflection of
Elohim's glory and the exact likeness of *Jehovah-Shammah's* being.
_____ has no worries, because *Jehovah-Jesus* holds everything together.
_____ exalts *Jehovah-Jesus*, who after he had cleansed people from
their sins, received the highest position, next to our Father in heaven.
_____ has joy because his/her body is *Jehovah's*
temple and his Spirit lives in _____.
_____ is one of *Jehovah-Shammah's* people.
Thankfully, _____'s body is the temple of the living *Jehovah-Shammah*,
because he lives and walks among us.
Jehovah-Shammah is always with _____.

Amen.

✝

JEHOVAH-SHAMMAH IN THE FLESH

(Based on the promises found in Romans 8)

_____ rejoices as there is no condemnation for those who dwell in *Jehovah-Jesus.*
_____ is now under the Spirit of life and has been
set free from the law of sin and death.
_____ worships *Jehovah-Shammah,* who sent his own Son,
Jehovah-Jesus, in a body with the likeness of man.
Jehovah-Jesus sacrificed his life on the cross and paid for all _____'s sins,
ending its control over _____.
_____, with all confidence, cries out, "Abba, Father," because
Jehovah-Shammah now abides in _____.
_____ considers all the sufferings of this present time not worth
comparing to the glory that will be revealed to _____.
_____ loves *Jehovah-Shammah* and knows
that all things work together for good
in accordance with his amazing purposes.
Jehovah-Shammah foreknew _____ and predestined him/her to be conformed
to the image of his Son, *Jehovah-Jesus.*
Jehovah-Shammah predestined, called, and justified _____.
Those whom *Jehovah-Shammah* vindicated, like _____, he also glorified.
If *Jehovah-Shammah* is for _____, no one can be against _____.
_____ knows that *Jehovah-Shammah,* who did not spare his own Son,
but gave him up for _____, will also graciously give _____ all things.
_____ is sure that neither death nor life, nor angels nor rulers, nor things
present nor things to come, nor powers, nor height nor depth, nor anything else in
all creation, will be able to separate _____ from the love of *Jehovah-Shammah.*

Amen.

†

JEHOVAH-SHAMMAH IS THERE

_____ rejoices, as the name *Jehovah-Shammah* means

Jehovah is there and intimately with _____.

_____ rests in the knowledge, as each Hebrew name of God

reveals a deeper dimension and understanding of *Jehovah*,

that *Jehovah-Shammah* is the perfect name

to climax the Old Testament revelations of *Elohim*.

_____ is thankful that

Jehovah-Shammah's name represents the promise and pledge of

the completion of _____'s purpose and final rest—

to glorify *Jehovah* and enjoy him forever.

_____ will never be forsaken nor forgotten by *Jehovah-Shammah*,

because *Jehovah-Jesus* paid the price for all the payment for his/her sins.

_____ rests in his/her joyful reconciliation with *Jehovah*.

_____ worships *Jehovah-Shammah*, as this name points to

and has been fulfilled perfectly in the Savior of the world, *Jehovah-Jesus*.

_____ looks forward to the day when our King,

Jehovah-Jesus, comes again in all his glory.

_____ will then see the full, complete, and

extraordinary expression of *Jehovah-Shammah*.

_____ is thankful that the great *Elohim* is with _____ because

Jehovah-Shammah dwells with _____.

_____ is *Jehovah-Shammah's* child, and

Jehovah is _____'s *Elohim*.

Amen.

†

My Prayers to Jehovah-Shammah

"I am an **Elohim** who is near. I am also an **Elohim** who is far
away," declares **Yahweh** [**Jehovah**]. "No one can hide so that I can't
see him," declares **Yahweh** [**Jehovah**]. ~ Jeremiah 23:23–24

BEFORE WE BEGIN praying to our ever-present *Jehovah-Shammah*, let's
take a breath and inhale the power that resides in our omnipresent
Jehovah. When invoking the name *Jehovah-Shammah*, we declare to
ourselves and all within hearing distance that our great *Jehovah* is always there,
protecting us, and will never abandon us.

1. As we focus on *Jehovah-Shammah* and his continual presence, how does
   knowing that the mightiest force and being in the universe is always with
   us alter your prayer request?

   ....

   ....

   ....

   ....

   ....

2. Does understanding that you are praying to *Jehovah-Shammah*, who gave up his greatest treasure, his Son, *Jehovah-Jesus*, for you and therefore will not withhold any good gift from you, comfort you? Why or why not?

_____

_____

_____

3. List your prayer requests to our *Jehovah-Shammah*, who is the promise and pledge of the completion of the purpose of all of our final rest, which is to glorify *Jehovah* and enjoy him:

_____

_____

_____

4. Record your praises to your *Jehovah-Shammah*, your mighty and extraordinary *Elohim* and Savior, before he answers your prayers, despite your situation:

_____

_____

_____

_____

Every good gift and every perfect gift is from above, from the Father who made the sun, moon, and stars. The Father doesn't change like the shifting shadows produced by the sun and the moon. (James 1:17)

Prayer Summary

"But when you pray, go into your room and shut the door and
pray to your Father who is in secret. And your Father who
sees in secret will reward you." ~ Matthew 6:6 ESV

P RAYER IS A simple, authentic, and honest conversation with God.
According to writer and author L. B. Cowman, prayer "connects us
with God. This is the bridge that spans every gulf and bears us over
every abyss of danger or of need."[62]

I challenge you to pray BIG, crazy prayers. These fervent prayers, just like
the ones the church offered up in Acts 12:5–16, brought forth an angel of *Elohim*
to free Peter from prison, loosening the chains that bound him to two soldiers,
and enabled him to walk undetected past all the guards and through the iron
city gates. In awe of *Jehovah's* power, Peter found himself in front of the same
home where the gathering of saints interceded for his rescue.

What if you could have that same access to *Elohim*, the Creator of the
universe? Thankfully, you can. Verbally declaring that Jesus Christ is your
Lord and Savior, admitting you are a sinner, and acknowledging your need for
Jehovah-Jesus to come into your heart and take control of your life now reconciles you with *Elohim*—you are saved from his wrath. This is a gift and is not
dependent on what you have or have not done. Through your acceptance that
your salvation has been paid for you by the complete work on the cross, you
now have access to eternal life with *Jehovah-Jesus*. And you can boldly approach
Jehovah-Elohim, the most powerful being in all creation, with your requests.

Since *Jehovah* already knows our hearts and deepest desires, it's not as if we
are revealing anything new to him. Presenting our petitions to *El-Shaddai* is a

sign of our dependency upon our all-sufficient *Jehovah*. Our *Jehovah-Tsidkenu* desires you to take that first step in humility and reach out to him.

Pray like you are speaking directly with your loving, all-powerful, eternal Abba or Daddy. Start journaling your dreams. These are the seeds *Jehovah-Rohi* planted in you. The very visions your *Jehovah-Rohi* wants to cultivate in and through you. Receive comfort that *Jehovah-Shammah* is here with you, surrounding and protecting you.

The very act of prayer identifies and specifically glorifies our *Adonai*. And like any loving father, our *Jehovah-Jireh*, who has prevision, delights in blessing us by answering our prayers exceedingly and abundantly beyond our wildest dreams.

Know that every trial, every season of suffering, and every trauma that comes upon you or your loved ones is also one of testing, sanctification, and transformation—to make you into a more accurate reflection of *Jehovah-Jesus*, our Savior. Trust in *Jehovah-Elohim* during these times. Rest in the knowledge that if *El-Shaddai* is showing you your sin, he wants you to turn from it, lay it on his altar or at the foot of the cross, repent (which means to apologize, ask for forgiveness, turn from doing it again), and offer restitution if possible. Remember, there is no condemnation for those in Christ Jesus (Romans 8:1) and all your sins are paid for on the cross. The blood of Christ as *Jehovah-Tsidkenu* exponentially covers you and your sins so *Jehovah-Jesus* can present you spotless and blameless to your holy and perfect *Elohim* as a righteous and purified offering.

After you receive these truths found in Scripture on the meaning of the names of God and his deep, intimate care of you, just breathe and receive his Holy Spirit. For you can now rejoice (see Philippians 4:4)—you are washed clean! The punishment of sin no longer remains on you! You are now able to approach the throne of *Elohim* with the confidence that your *Jehovah* does not withhold any good gift from those who walk uprightly (Psalm 84:11).

Again, I encourage you to rejoice!

Hebrew Names of God Summary

FOR THOSE OF you (like me) who enjoy swimming in the deep end of the theological pool, here's your flotation device in the form of the Hebrew names of God as defined by *Strong's Exhaustive Concordance* and *Brown-Driver-Briggs* (BDB), a Hebrew-English Dictionary.

1. Elohim: The TRUE, supreme God. This also refers to angels, exceedingly, very great, and mighty. Occasionally, this name is used as a way of deference to magistrates and sometimes as rulers, judges, either as divine representatives at sacred places or as reflecting divine majesty and power.[63]

2. Jehovah, the Lord: YHVH is derived from the Hebrew word *hayah* (meaning to exist). *Yahweh* or *Jehovah* means the self-Existent or Eternal and the Jewish national name of God. The name is all-encompassing and represents the One bringing into being, life-giver, the One who is (meaning the absolute and unchangeable one). It also refers to all that his servants look for, the existing, ever-living, and the One ever-coming into manifestation as the God of redemption. Interestingly enough, the pronunciation *Jehovah* was unknown until 1520, when the Italian theologian Galatinus introduced it.[64]

3. El-Shaddai: A compound word of two Hebrew names, *El* and *Shaddai*. *El* means God, Mighty One, power, and strong. Shortened from *'ayil* (which represents strength and mighty), this Hebrew name of God especially points to the Almighty (but also used of any deity). *El* is a divine name and is seen in Scripture repeatedly as the holy God, One only and true God of Israel, my God, the great God, the faithful God, the God who is my rock, God of my fathers, the God of heaven, the God who is the joy of my triumph, the God who lets himself be seen, the God of glory, the all-knowing God, the everlasting God, a compassionate God, a forgiving God, a gracious God, a jealous God, a living God, and God is with us.[65]

Shaddai means almighty, my sovereign lord, and omnipotent. It originates from the root Hebrew word *shadad*, which means to deal violently with, despoil, devastate, ruin.[66]

4. Adonai: or *Adonay*. This precious Hebrew name refers to my Lord or the Lord when used as a proper name of God. An emphatic or unequivocal form of *'adown* representing a lord, master, or owner.[67]

5. Jehovah-Jireh: or *Yhvh Yireh*. *Jehovah* will see to it. Also, a symbolic name for Mount Moriah. From the two Hebrew words, *Yhovah* means *Jehovah*, the Lord, and *ra'ah* or *raah* to see.[68] When both names are combined, it means the One who has prevision because *Jehovah* has always existed and therefore presees and provides for our needs before we are even aware of them.

6. Jehovah-Rophe: *Jehovah*, the existing one who heals you. *Rophe* or *raphe*, which means to heal or be healed entirely. In Scripture, *rophe* as a noun means a physician, and as a verb, it means to darn, mend, repair, pacify, reappear, take care, and stitch together. It also means becoming fresh or purified. It can refer to the healing of an individual's distresses and illness, as well as curing the hurts of a nation through restoration, favor, and forgiveness.[69]

7. Jehovah-Nissi: *Jehovah* is my banner. *Jehovah-Nissi* is the symbolic name of Moses's altar in the desert. The name is from the Hebrew words *Yhovah* meaning *Jehovah*, the Lord, and *nes*, which is a flag, banner, standard, pole, ensign, signal, or sign.[70]

8. Jehovah-M'Kaddesh: *Jehovah* who sanctifies. *M'Kaddesh* is a form of the Hebrew verb *qadash*, which means to be set apart or consecrated. Consecrated means to become or declare holy, transmit or manifest holiness, or dedicate or purify oneself or something, usually unto *Jehovah*.[71]

9. Jehovah-Shalom: *Jehovah* is peace. *Jehovah-Shalom* is also the name of an altar Gideon built for *Jehovah* in Palestine (see Judges 6:24). This name of God is a derivative from the two Hebrew words, *Yhovah* meaning *Jehovah*, the Lord, and *shalom* (from *shalam*) meaning safe, well, favor, friend, great, good health, and perfect.[72]

10. Jehovah-Tsidqenu: or *Jehovah-Tsidkenu*. *Jehovah* is our righteousness. It is also the name for Jerusalem and the Messiah—the Lord our righteousness. From the two Hebrew words *Yhovah* (*Jehovah*, the Lord) and *tsedeq* (justice, righteous cause).[73]

11. Jehovah-Rohi: or *Roi* or *Ra'ah*. *Jehovah* is my Shepherd. From the two Hebrew words *Yhovah* meaning *Jehovah*, the Lord, and *Rohi*, *Roi*, or *Ra'ah*, which implies to pasture, tend, and graze. It also refers to a ruler or teacher of people (as pastor/shepherd and his flock).[74]

12. Jehovah-Shammah: *Jehovah* is thither or there; *Jehovah-Shammah*, a symbolic title of Jerusalem. From *Yhovah* meaning *Jehovah*, the Lord, and *sham,* which means everywhere, here, or there.[75]

Notes from the Author

WRITING THIS PRAYER book blessed me beyond measure. Every time I wrote a section, I would walk away with a deeper, if not sweeter, sense of God and his love, protection, and provision for his children. I almost didn't want to finish it!

Here is a list of a few of the things I found interesting throughout my research on the names of God and the scriptural meaning behind each one:

1. As I created personalized prayers from Scripture and attempted to make them understandable and applicable, I felt like I was restoring, or rather updating, some beautiful yet mighty artifact. I believe our *Jehovah* wants us to return to a daily communion and conversation with him.
2. The chronological order of the Hebrew names of God as listed in our Bible evolves from universal to personal, or rather intimate, as we travel through Scripture and get to know the faithfulness of our amazing *Jehovah* better.
3. God's revelation of his names directly correlates to increasing our need and affection for him.
4. I loved how each Hebrew name directly points to our Savior. Jesus was not the contingency arrangement; rather, he was *always* the plan. *Elohim* knew how much we would need a Redeemer when he created heaven, earth, and humanity. In *Jehovah-Tsidkenu's* righteousness, he providentially planned a way back for us to come into his presence through his Son, *Jehovah-Jesus*.
5. Gratefully, as *Jehovah-Jireh* provides for us, our *Jehovah-Rophe* heals us, and *Jehovah-Nissi* is our miracle, while *Jehovah-M'Kaddesh* sanctifies us so we can easily approach our holy God. *Jehovah-Shalom* gives us his peace, *Jehovah-Tsidkenu* covers us with his righteousness, and *Jehovah-Rohi* comforts us, as *Jehovah-Shammah* never leaves us nor forsakes us. This

extraordinary spectrum of love, grace, and protection completely covers us as only our great *Jehovah* can.

6. Our *El-Shaddai* and *Adonai* is a mighty and merciful God.

7. *But God...*But prayer.

Acknowledgments

My *Jehovah-Jesus*—everything I do is through him. I would never have attempted to write this prayer book if it wasn't for his constant prompting and his saints who have encouraged me to finish this work. I am continually in awe of him.

My husband—you are my greatest supporter, editor, and most faithful partner. I am so grateful to *Elohim* that he saw fit to unite us as husband and wife. I don't believe I could have accomplished all that I have without your unending and tireless support.

My children—you both are extraordinary, and I thank *Jehovah* for the honor of being your mother. Writing books takes sacrifice—actually, anything worthwhile does—and I am humbled that you two released me to be obedient to the calling of our great and merciful *El-Shaddai*.

My editors—Christy, Kimberly, and Pam—you all make me look good. And for David Lang, I couldn't have accurately translated any of the Names of God into pointed Hebrew if it wasn't for you. You all are the supple polishing cloth over my tarnished works that make this book shine and reflect the glory of our *Jehovah*.

Kevin and Yvette Kendrick—praising God for Kevin's miraculous recovery from COVID-19. I am still in awe of God and so grateful he woke me up in the middle of the night to tell me to write this book on praying personalized scripture the day before we all interceded to *Jehovah-Rophe* for Kevin. Yvette, thank you for reaching out to friends to pray over Zoom for your husband. That was one anointed and healing webinar!

My readers—thank you so much for your encouragement, prayers, and support to keep writing. Our *Jehovah-Nissi* uses each one of you to blow fresh wind into my sails. Thank you.

Recipients of my message of HOPE through Lift Your Gaze—your pain, and desire to forgive and move closer to *Jehovah-Jesus*, challenges me. I am indebted to you and your prayers.

To God be all the glory!

About the Author

Kim M. Clark is the award-winning publisher of Deep Waters Books and has authored the Amazon best-selling and multiple-award-winning book, *Deep Waters: Lift Your Gaze,* the supporting award-winning devotional, *Deep Waters: Lift Your Gaze 30-Day Devotional*, and the devotional in Spanish, *Aguas profundas: Levanta Tu Mirada*. She believes this prayer book on the Hebrew names of God is by far her most anointed book yet.

To offer hope to those experiencing trauma, Kim founded Lift Your Gaze, a 501(c)3 organization, where she shares her message of hope across the globe.

Kim has run two marathons, with respectable times, despite the angry protests from her knees. She and her family enjoy living in the Florida sunshine and playing outdoor sports, especially ones with their active 105-pound yellow lab who identifies as a tiny lap dog but has a bark loud enough to terrify every delivery person who dares to ring the doorbell.

To schedule Kim for highly interactive, energetic, and hope-filled speaking engagements, email Kim's team at info@kimmclark.com or scan the QR code below.

Thank You

A portion of the proceeds from this publication provides HOPE through Lift Your Gaze, a 501(c)3 organization.

For more information on Lift Your Gaze's initiatives, visit www.liftyourgaze.org or scan the QR code below.

Thank you for your support and your gift of light.

May the LORD *[Jehovah]* bless you and protect you,
May the LORD *[Jehovah]* smile upon you and be gracious to you.
May the LORD *[Jehovah]* show you his favor and give you his peace.
~ Numbers 6:24–26 NLT

Endnotes

1   https://www.merriam-webster.com/dictionary/prayer, accessed 3-22-21.
2   https://www.merriam-webster.com/dictionary/pray, accessed on 3-31-21.
3   https://www.worldinvisible.com/library/murray/helps_intercession/hi15.htm, accessed 5-4-21.
4   Nathan Stone, *Names of God* (Chicago: Moody Publishers, 2010), 10–14.
5   https://www.biblestudytools.com/bible-study/topical-studies/yeshua-deliverer-savior.html, accessed 1-6-22.
6   Nathan Stone, *Names of God* (Chicago: Moody Publishers, 2010), 31.
7   Ibid., 117.
8   Ibid., 27.
9   Ibid., 26.
10 Ibid., 31.
11 https://www.lexico.com/en/definition/omnipotent, accessed 4-1-21.
12 https://archive.org/stream/brethrenevangeli78150bens/brethrenevangeli78150bens_djvu.txt, accessed 3-24-22.
13 Stone, *Names of God* (2010), 33.
14 Ibid., 36.
15 Ibid., 42.
16 Ibid., 37.
17 https://www.lexico.com/definition/eternal, accessed 5-17-21.
18 Rev. A. B. *Simpson, Days of Heaven Upon Earth: A Year Book of Scripture Texts and Living Truths*, (Nyack, NY: Christian Alliance Publishing Co.), 320.
19 Stone, *Names of God* (2010), 52.
20 Ibid., 51.
21 Ibid., 54.
22 Ibid., 60.
23 https://www.lexico.com/en/definition/omnipotent, accessed 5-19-21.
24 https://www.spurgeongems.org/chsbm12.pdf , accessed 3-24-22.
25 Stone, *Names of God* (2010), 62.

26   Ibid., 63.

27   Ibid., 65.

28   Ibid., 64.

29   Ibid., 72.

30   https://www.goodreads.com/author/quotes/1148687.Samuel_Chadwick, accessed 3-24-22.

31   Ibid., 79.

32   Ibid., 85–86.

33   https://integratedcatholiclife.org/2014/03/daily-catholic-quote-from-peter-kreeft-5/, accessed 5-3-21.

34   Stone, *Names of God* (2010), 97.

35   https://www.lexico.com/en/definition/healer, accessed 4-21-21

36   Compiled by Mrs. Chas. E. Cowman, Farrar, *Streams in the Desert* (Los Angeles, The Oriental Mission Society, 1947), 318.

37   Stone, *Names of God* (2010), 109.

38   Ibid., 116.

39   https://www.newworldencyclopedia.org/entry/Abba, accessed 4-1-21.

40   https://www.lexico.com/en/definition/protector, accessed 4-1-21.

41   https://www.johnnewton.org/Articles/371427/The_John_Newton/new_menus/Hymns/OH_Book_2/OH_Book_2.aspx, accessed 7-3-21.

42   Stone, *Names of God* (2010), 119.

43   Ibid, 124.

44   Ibid., 128.

45   https://www.merriam-webster.com/dictionary/sanctifies, accessed 9-27-21.

46   Stone, *Names of God* (2010), 122.

47   Stone, *Names of God* (2010), 143.

48   Ibid., 137.

49   Ibid., 138.

50   Ibid.

51   Ibid., 145.

52   https://www.worldinvisible.com/library/murray/5bm.10353/5bm.10353.22.htm, accessed, 3-24-22.

53   Stone, *Names of God* (2010). 149.

54   Ibid., 158.

55   https://prayer-coach.com/prayer-quotes-charles-spurgeon/, accessed 11-1-21.

56   Stone, *Names of God* (2010), 163.

57   Ibid., 164.

58   Ibid., 166.

59   https://www.biblegateway.com/passage/?search=Psalm+91+&version=VOICE, accessed 4-17-21.

60   Stone, *Names of God* (2010), 178.

61   Ibid., 179.

62   https://www.crosswalk.com/devotionals/desert/streams-in-the-desert-

november-2nd.html, accessed 2-8-22.

63 https://biblehub.com/hebrew/430.htm, accessed 6-28-21.

64 https://biblehub.com/hebrew/3068.htm, accessed 6-28-21.

65 https://biblehub.com/hebrew/410.htm, accessed 6-28-21.

66 https://biblehub.com/hebrew/7706.htm, accessed 6-28-21.

67 https://biblehub.com/hebrew/136.htm, accessed 6/28/21.

68 https://biblehub.com/strongs/hebrew/3070.htm, accessed 6/28/21.

69 https://biblehub.com/hebrew/7495.htm, accessed 6/28/21.

70 https://biblehub.com/hebrew/3071.htm, accessed 6/28/21.

71 https://biblehub.com/hebrew/6942.htm, accessed 8-19-21.

72 https://biblehub.com/hebrew/3073.htm, accessed 6-28-21.

73 https://biblehub.com/hebrew/3072.htm, accessed 6-28-21.

74 https://biblehub.com/hebrew/7462.htm, accessed 6-28-21.

75 https://biblehub.com/hebrew/3074.htm, accessed 6-28-21.